reflections
ON PRACTICE

Other titles in the series

Language teaching in the mirror
edited by Antony Peck and David Westgate
REFLECTIONS ON PRACTICE 1

This book focuses on the why and how of reflecting on classroom practice. Different modes demonstrated include: evaluations; diary keeping; video action-replay; peer observation; micro-teaching. The final chapter provides guidelines on how to develop a theoretical framework for action research and the practical steps to setting up a project.

Reflections on reading: from GCSE to 'A' level
edited by Mike Grenfell
REFLECTIONS ON PRACTICE 2

> Three practising teachers consider approaches to reading in a foreign language at intermediate and advanced level in schools and colleges. The first charts the reading habits of a Year 9 class; the other two look at the problems learners face between GCSE and 'A' level and explore strategies which can help to overcome the difficulties.

Reflections on modern languages in primary education: six case studies
edited by Alison Hurrell and Peter Satchwell
REFLECTIONS ON PRACTICE 3

> Six teachers consider, among other aspects, progression from primary to secondary, integrating the foreign language into the primary curriculum and teaching in two languages.

Reflections on the target language
Peter S Neil
REFLECTIONS ON PRACTICE 4

> This book examines the use of the TL by ten teachers of German who were preparing their pupils for KS4. It analyses the TL from the teachers' and researchers' standpoint and also looks at the pupils' perceptions of their teachers' use of the TL and of their own language-learning problems.

reflections
ON PRACTICE

Series editor: Richard Johnstone

Reflections on grammar-implicit language teaching

Margaret Wells

CiLT
Centre for Information
on Language Teaching and Research

The views expressed in this book are those of the author and do not necessarily reflect the views of CILT.

REFLECTIONS ON PRACTICE

Editorial Committee
Professor Richard Johnstone, University of Stirling
Professor Chris Brumfit, University of Southampton
Professor Michael Byram, University of Durham
Ute Hitchin, CILT
Dr Lid King, CILT
Paul Meara, University College of Swansea
Dr Rosamond Mitchell, University of Southampton
Antony Peck, University of York
David Westgate, University of Newcastle-upon-Tyne

First published 2000
by the Centre for Information on Language Teaching and Research (CILT)
20 Bedfordbury, London WC2N 4LB

Copyright © 2000 Centre for Information on Language Teaching and Research
ISBN 1 902031 43 1

A catalogue record for this book is available from the British Library

All rights reserved. No part of this publication may be reproduced, stored in a retrieval system, or transmitted by any other means, electronic, mechanical, photocopying, recording or otherwise without prior permission in writing from CILT or under licence from the Copyright Licensing Agency Limited, of 90 Tottenham Court Road, London W1T 4LP.

Margaret Wells has asserted her right to be identified as author of this work, in accordance with the Copyright, Designs and Patents Act, 1988.

Typeset by Karin Erskine
Printed in Great Britain by Copyprint UK Ltd

CILT Publications are available from: **Central Books,** 99 Wallis Rd, London E9 5LN. Tel: 0845 458 9910. Fax: 0845 458 9912. Book trade representation (UK and Ireland): **Broadcast Book Services,** Charter House, 27a London Road, Croydon CR0 2RE. Tel: 020 8681 8949. Fax: 020 8688 0615.

Contents

Introduction *Richard Johnstone*   1

Chapter 1 Reflections and research   3
Understanding the new approach to MFL teaching   3
The NC methodology and its implications for the classroom   4
Preparing for action research   6

Chapter 2 The place and role of 'grammar' in the explicit/implicit debate   9
Native language (L1) acquisition and foreign language (FL or L2) learning:
defining these different concepts   9
Some arguments in support of the use of naturalistic teaching styles
in relation to L2   13
Explicit (G-E) and implicit (G-I) procedures   15

Chapter 3 The action research (AR) plan   20
Preparing to activate the grammar-teaching principle   21
The agenda, materials and strategies used for teaching GCSE French
by the selected (NC) methods   24
Consolidating the principal essential constituents of teaching method   28

Chapter 4 Grammar-implicit (G-I) teaching in action   31
The teaching programme in Year 9   31
Lessons featuring learner-centred activities   47
The AR teaching methods (M1 and M2) in practice: summary and conclusion   52

Chapter 5 The teachers' attitudes and perspectives during the AR   56
The responses of the AR teachers to their grammar-implicit teaching brief   56
The teachers' feedback on their experience in the classroom   57
Conclusion to the teachers' discussions   68

Chapter 6 The responses of the AR learners   71
A selection of questionnaires and the learners' responses   71
Comments on the overall enquiry into the learners' responses   92

Chapter 7 The subject outcomes attained by the AR learners   **96**

Evaluating the AR through the performances of the learners   96
The results in Year 9   97
The results in Year 10   101
The results in Year 11   103
The results of the 1994 GCSE examination in French   106
Reflections on the outcomes of the AR and its impact on the learners
and their performances   108

Chapter 8 Evaluating the grammar-implicit (G-I) principle   **110**

The conditions needed for the appropriate delivery of the G-I teaching mode   110
The G-I teaching approach used by the AR teaching team   111
Final personal reflections   115

Endpiece   *David Westgate*   **117**

Appendix A   Samples of the AR pupils' creative work   **121**

Appendix B   A selection of key background sources   **131**

This volume in the *Reflections on Practice* series is dedicated to
all teachers and learners in Modern Foreign Languages classrooms.

Acknowledgements

I happily express my thanks to the people named below for the various parts that they played in the production of this book and in the action research which preceded it.

The 'Task Force' of teachers and learners, who applied my methodological experiment to their work between the years 1991 and 1994. I shall remember our shared experience with lasting affection.

Richard Johnstone and David Westgate, for their articles flanking my report, for their support of my book generally and for their earlier encouragement of my research effort.

Ute Hitchin (representing CILT), for editing my first book and providing insights to carry forward, potentially.

Margaret Wells

Key to abbreviations

The abbreviations which are explained below are used in this book. Those marked with an asterisk (*) appertain specifically to the research programme which is described.

NEAB	Northern Examination and Assessment Board
MFL	Modern Foreign Languages
FL	Foreign Languages
L1	first (native) language
L2	second language
NC	National Curriculum
AR (*)	Action Research
M (*)	'Method' (used in the AR programme)
Factor X (*)	extension of the method = summaries of foreign language grammar, made in English
M1 (*)	pure 'Method' = M
M2 (*)	M + X = 'Method' (M) combined with grammar summaries (factor X)
G-I (*)	grammar-implicit foreign language teaching; or M or M1
G-E (*)	grammar-explicit foreign language teaching; or M2 (using the factor X)
TL	target language

Introduction

CILT's *Reflections on Practice* gives an opportunity to practitioners of language teaching or languages teacher education not only to reflect on aspects of their practice that they consider to be important but also to share this in writing with readers of the series.

At present there is no more central a topic in school modern languages departments than the teaching and learning of grammar. The feeling has gained ground that communicative approaches, whatever their merits, do not sit altogether easily with current imperatives to maximise students' national examination performance. Grammar teaching has therefore made a come-back.

However, very little evidence has been carefully and systematically collected in contemporary UK school classrooms in relation to how learners acquire not just knowledge about grammar but, more importantly, a functional competence in grammar that enables them in practice to be both accurate and creative. It is understandable therefore that among teachers and teacher educators there should be different notions as to how this may be achieved.

It is highly appropriate that *Reflections on Practice* should address this important topic and that Margaret Wells should be the person to write about it. When she was a busy Head of Department in a comprehensive secondary school in the north-east of England, preparing her students for the GCSE examination, Margaret was also undertaking PhD research at the University of Newcastle-upon-Tyne under the supervision of David Westgate. The focus of Margaret's doctoral research was her students' learning of grammar.

Having had the pleasure of reading Margaret's full PhD thesis, I was keen that she should have the further opportunity – energy permitting! – to distil her thoughts and present them in a somewhat different way for the benefit of a wider professional readership. This she has achieved in the present publication.

There are several things about Margaret's achievement that I find impressive. These include: her tenacity in reconciling the demands of being a busy Head of Department with those of simultaneously pursuing doctoral research; the insight that enabled her to develop a view about grammar learning that ran somewhat against the tide of received wisdom; her success in obtaining highly relevant classroom evidence; her ability to present her thoughts and her findings in a way that satisfies the demands of professional scholarship – and above all, her commitment as a teacher to continue asking serious questions about her own practice and to finding answers that suited the context in which she was working.

Professor Richard Johnstone
Series Editor: REFLECTIONS ON PRACTICE

Chapter 1

Reflections and research

Understanding the new approach to Modern Foreign Languages (MFL) teaching

For all of us who teach foreign languages in schools, the new National Curriculum (NC) teaching approach expresses preferences for the comprehensive application of the target language (TL) and for the grammatical agenda to be left embedded and undeclared. This was, at least, my personal reading of the NC intention, as my colleagues and I began preparing our investigation of the advocated methods immediately upon receiving the documents of 1990 and then those of 1992. These were the initial Proposal and the Non-Statutory Guidance respectively. We wanted to gain a perspective on the practicability, efficiency and effectiveness of the implied procedures and processes in relation to our learners. We quickly discovered that a major part of the exercise was the matter of defining and planning those procedures and processes themselves, before they could be viewed in action.

Our interpretation of the NC policy for MFL and its influence upon my work within the department was informed by the texts which contain the method criteria. They are taken from the DES Proposal of 1990 (which also influenced the later Non-Statutory Guidance) and are as follows:

(i) that there should be a grammatical content which is provided implicitly, as an integral part of the teaching syllabus, and taught by naturalistic methods (DES 1990, 10.8) echoing primary practice:

'Learners of all abilities are much more likely to be able to grasp and work with grammatical structures if these are presented not through formal exposition but through demonstrations which make strong visual or aural impressions ...' (9.17) and

(ii) that the agenda, which is the TL, should also be delivered in the target language:

'It is evident that such (grammatical) demonstrations can quite naturally be carried out in the target language' (9.18); that further:

4 — REFLECTIONS ON GRAMMAR-IMPLICIT LANGUAGE TEACHING

> 'The natural use of the TL for virtually all communication is a sure sign of a good modern languages course. Learners are enabled to see that the language is not only the object of study but also an effective medium for conducting the normal business of the classroom.' (10.7)

My Modern Languages department was made ready for the application of a 'grammar-implicit' (G-I) teaching plan – the shape and consistency of which were to be decided – and for the comprehensive use of the TL in all our classes, in literal response to the above-quoted policy clauses. Then, in support of my need to align the G-I inquiry with a contrasting teaching strategy, I established the 'grammar-explicit' (G-E) principle from the advice given in the policy clause, which I perceived to be:

(iii) conceding the use of occasional summaries of grammatical content, made in the native language, in order to clarify and consolidate the matter taught:

> 'Teachers may nevertheless judge that a brief explanation in English ... would help understanding ...' (9.18) '... though the value of grammar notes, dictated by the teacher and written down by the learner, is held in some doubt ...' (9.19)

Thus emerged a factor X, an explicit grammar teaching principle for use in forming G-E. This would contrast with the G-I format by explaining grammar in **summaries** delivered in English and, for our purposes, it would indeed be accompanied by dictated and written-down notes. We practised these methods, between the years 1991 and 1994, in a dummy-run to the NC, and measured the effects of our teaching efforts as reflected in our pupils' learning outcomes and their attitudes to their work in the methodological contexts.

The NC methodology and its implications for the classroom

In the context of our own work, my colleagues and I quickly realised that there were direct difficulties for all of us, once we put into effect our decision to take the selected policy clauses literally and teach unconditionally by the G-I method, using the TL exclusively. Of course, we had already accustomed ourselves to using a considerable amount of the TL in our teaching during the ten or more years which have accommodated the GCSE and the Joint 16+, and which carried forward some influence from the former CSE (the first system to turn its back on 'prose' translation and, later, on 'unseen' translation also).

We were then, as now, of necessity engaged with the growing communicative agenda and purpose of Modern Languages teaching, which we attempted to articulate through a communicative teaching approach involving a 'kinder' relationship with grammar and a sustained multi-purpose, though not necessarily exclusive, application of the TL. Indeed, in my department, we all admitted to using English when we felt it to be appropriate or when all else failed, in order to explain vocabulary terms, difficult sequences in 'comprehensions' and for most grammatical structures. On our own 'bad days' as well as those of our classes, we felt entitled to use English (the L1), in order to maintain the dynamic and dynamism of our lessons. This permitted flexibility took the stress and worry out of the teaching of the trickier matters of our agenda. It eased the burden of our responsibility and the tensions which were inevitably generated out of our sense of accountability to the learners, their linguistic development and the outcomes of their learning.

Then, all of a sudden, there we were, deciding on a rigid methodological formula for use in our classrooms! We pledged ourselves to shun all temptations to compromise our decisions, except within the framework of our formally devised G-E teaching approach, the enabler of my intended contrastive study. My colleagues and I were all products of 'grammar-translation' education in Modern Languages terms, despite the 20 years or more which separated me, the oldest, from them. We all suspected, therefore, that the cut-and-dried decision to trial G-I, all in the target language, would quickly prove to have two forms of reality: the one as a laudable theory and the other as a complex and exasperating practice.

We knew at the outset that we were giving ourselves an ambitious exercise to perform and to sustain over a long period of time. The task was made all the harder because of the 'do or die' spirit which we attached to it and because we were using the designed teaching structures in **live** situations featuring large numbers of **real** learners, a full and **real** MFL syllabus, a **real** work setting, targeting **real** results for our pupils. The project of our making an exploratory incursion into processes of MFL teaching methods may have formed into a neat and possibly praiseworthy rehearsal of the NC's formalised expectations, later. However, this rehearsal was the learners' **one and only opportunity** to dispatch this compulsory study with the best prospects for success. This was their entitlement and it placed them in the hands of their teachers and the teaching plans. Enough said, except that we teachers carried a full awareness of this situation with us as we journeyed through our teaching course (1991–1994). We appraised the developments systematically and applied care and consideration in our work as never before!

It soon emerged that there were, indeed, implications for the classroom business and for the teachers, once the method G-I was put in place. Clearly, these affected G-E also, which echoed G-I and differed only in the annexed area of the factor X, ie the use of retrospective grammar summary delivered in the native language (L1). The lengthy list of the issues which arose included the following questions which begged discussion:

- What does one really mean by 'grammar-implicit' (G-I)? What is the nature of 'grammar-explicit' (G-E)? What are the principal differences between them?

What have (the) writers and researchers reported on these concepts, in theory and/or through practice? Has research offered a perspective on the ongoing debate for the practising teacher and the work of the classroom?

- How can G-E be conceived and articulated in the syllabus and in lesson plans?

- What appear to be the likely implications of trialling a strictly controlled teaching approach for the learners and the learning processes and, later, for the course outcomes reflected in the learners' results?

- What are the effects on teachers' classroom – and group – management? On teacher/pupil rapport and inter-group relationships?

- Could there be a cost in terms of all-important learners' self confidence and motivation?

- What are the implications for the teachers' subject-mastery; their ownership of agenda; the issues of (disguised) didacticism/autonomy/ sharing and negotiation of agendas (all of which play a role in current classroom practice and procedures)?

- What consideration must be given to matters of lesson-structure; knowledge-building; pupil-profiling?

- What repercussions, if any, could emerge in terms of pupils' concentration; their subject management; their levels of general discipline and their teachers' responses to these matters?

I will allude to these issues in later chapters, in which I offer a fuller commentary on the principal aspects of the action research and its outcomes.

Preparing for action research (AR)

My department's acceptance of the NC's immediate (1990) challenge to teachers to use the teaching methods advocated in their policy necessitated that we prepared our minds with an appropriate understanding of our brief. This meant using 'borrowed' knowledge, **before** putting in the three trial years of teaching the GCSE course in French (1991 to 1994), but also **during** the whole of this time which prefaced the formal inception of the NC orders. Extensive research through reading was in any case a major feature of my own role as a researcher who sought to furnish a formal PhD study out of the experimental work that we were engaged with. The ideas and opinions that I gathered throughout that continuous reading activity informed my management of the project, as well as the staff's relationship to it, and our understanding of it as a working brief at its various stages of development. My reading also kept me appreciative of the position of the learners, who had been put in a receptive mode of engagement with a subject that they had already experienced in a different way in the past, during their time at Middle School. They were suddenly required to resume and continue to pursue their foreign language work in the manner of their native language, as it were. We had no way of anticipating how they would react to this.

The broad reading which I refer to here, and which advised my relationship with my task, was an extension of that undertaken throughout my teaching years as a natural part of my subject interest and exploration of teaching method. It is partly represented in the literature appendix at the back of this book. However, this influence was not at all one which dictated the action research procedure – the NC did that! – but it allowed us to recognise and discuss matters of process and development which arose, systematically, in many forms. These included symptoms; obstacles; consistencies and inconsistencies; expectations and disappointments and many facets of the learners' psychology regarding their MFL subject activities. There was much to be discovered about the prospect of language learning in the adolescent period and especially, where we were concerned, the prospect of the teenagers' mental management of the foreign language grammar. For me there was no richer and more rewarding discussion on the collective subject than that which I enjoyed with my colleagues in the department. Our insights combined with those gained from the works I referenced over the time of the preparation and enactment of the action research and the extended period of reflection and writing that engrossed me then and later. I also found it interesting and satisfying that my action research provided, in its turn, a kind of silent feedback to the opinions and claims of published writers!

In addition to all else, I know that my teaching colleagues also found the classroom trials illuminating. In the first instance, they were required to pause and honestly think out their special route to the teaching, and remain true to it. Then they were required to pool their reflections on it in group discussions. (Our most important lessons and all of our discussions were audio-recorded for future reference.) For the first time in all of our personal histories we found ourselves with a range of opportunities to get into other teachers' minds and see others' perceptions of the common work. We discussed issues relating to the work itself; to the teaching methods defined for immediate AR use and in general; our concern for our pupils and their subject needs; and our vision and ability to deal appropriately with the range of matters which affected our practice. We anticipated that we would all emerge from the work the better off for having done it.

As well as the reading that we did in order to benefit our understanding of the 'grammar-implicit' notion and determine a teaching approach to satisfy it, we found a certain measure of support through in-service. This was partly externally organised and visited by us, partly internally 'bought in' and directed by recognised exponents, specifically for our AR purposes. On matters relating to MFL teaching, there is a continuing need for in-service informed through research.

8 — REFLECTIONS ON GRAMMAR-IMPLICIT LANGUAGE TEACHING

Summarising the Research Purpose and Design

The three-year GCSE examination course, followed through with our Year 9 intake of 1991, was underpinned by the NC teaching method, activating a 'grammar-implicit' approach (G-I), and became my research project. It was designed, engineered and managed by myself, enlisting an active contribution from my immediate colleagues in terms of their teaching input by G-I but without ever intending to increase their work load, other than possibly in terms of the time and effort spent on lesson preparation. The project was written up by myself on:

(a) a daily basis, as the experiment was put in place with the timetabled lessons;

(b) a half-termly basis, as the experiment gathered pace and generated patterns of development;

(c) a yearly basis, as stage-by-stage consolidation banked up; and

(d) at the conclusion of the three years' time-scale, when it was possible to assess the developments which had occurred in the project.

In the final analysis, the action research was cross-referenced with and interleaved with the historical research, (which represented its natural setting and the source from which it had evolved), and with the general reading of works pertaining to the collective MFL grammar-focused enquiry. My own 20 ledgers of evidence in written (and illustrated) report form; upwards of 50 audio-cassettes of recorded lessons and discussions; occasional video recordings of lessons; recorded and transcribed case-studies and interviews; 18 questionnaires with their digests, attesting to learners' attitudes, responses and reactions – all this evidence conveyed the action research to its point of encounter with the relevant reading, and with the writing up process itself. The resulting thesis was examined in 1997.

My finished work now enables me to subscribe to reflections on a number of Modern Languages curricular matters, but especially the one concerning **implicit grammar teaching**. I invite readers to observe, in the further chapters of this book, my department's experience in dealing with G-I and to reflect with us objectively and, one hopes, in some way productively, on relevant matters pertaining to the practice we have in common in National Curriculum terms and times.

Chapter 2

The place and role of 'grammar' in the explicit/implicit debate

Native language (L1) acquisition and foreign language (FL or L2) learning: defining these different concepts in the learners' educational context

No foreign language teacher needs to be told that the processes of learning the mother tongue and the foreign language are separated by essential differences. There are differences, therefore, in the teaching of them. These differences have their starting point in the conditions, circumstances and environments which surround the two types of language development.

Because the process of acquiring the mother tongue (L1) occurs uninterrupted and naturally in a **total** situation set in a whole time, whole space, whole community framework, it suits the term 'acquisition' by which it is known. The young individual, placed inside the native culture and language, is exposed to that language and responds to it, from the earliest stages of development. Being immersed, as it were, (s)he absorbs. Some writers, e.g. Krashen, Rivers, explain this process as one akin to 'osmosis', or 'through the pores'/'into the soul' learning. This is a process which happens, furthermore, in the majority of cases of 'immersion', whether the culture/language setting is directly native or not (Wilkins, 1974). The environment, in which individuals live, overtakes and swamps them. Smaller than their cultural context, they cannot resist or reject it but, instead, they have need of it in order to function, survive and grow. The native or quasi native language serves the individual's needs, enabling communication, the controlling of one's life, production, creativity and the expression of the emotions. Dodson (1967), Wilkinson (1971), Richards and Rodgers (1986) are representative of a range of writers who have clarified this relationship over time.

On the other hand, the foreign language (L2) is pursued outside its own cultural setting. It is a false reality, no matter how sensitively it is represented by those who teach it. It is usually brought to the child in the form of a discrete learning package – a school curriculum course – containing contrived targets which are negotiated in a classroom setting in which there are no equal partnerships and no equal sharing. In most cases, L2 learners have no compelling relationship with this course of learning, can express little or limited initiative in using it, could easily live without it and have difficulty, in fact, in living meaningfully with it. They lack the context, setting and circumstances which would make it relevant to their needs and necessitate their engagement with it to any significant degree. Indeed, it might be argued that many L2 learners of the pre-16 age range gain little more for their lives than an awareness of the existence in their world of another culture, which is expressed through a different tongue from their own.

This is, one might argue, at least a start. Even so, MFL remains a subject package which is placed before learners and their teachers by those who claim to know what is good for the former to learn and by what methods the latter should teach it. These two assumptions should be linked by an understanding of the processes by which the taught agenda is internalised by the learner, in order to produce the learning as the end product of the effort shared by learners in partnership with teachers. This understanding ought to inform:

(a) the 'grammar' agenda or syllabus, since not all of its elements are congruous with the stages of the development of the teenage learner (who nowadays has a shallow frame of reference in the L1); and

(b) the teaching methods which convey the 'grammar' to learners who are not substantially grammar-aware.

It has been accepted that L2 learning is a different process from L1 acquisition. We can now explore this divide further. The 'real', 'authentic', 'genuine' character of the L1 conditions are substituted in the L2 by 'realistic' and 'relevant' arrangements at best. Materials, texts, tasks, activities and realia are supplied to support the foreign language work, create a context and animate the learners' environment. MFL teachers transform their classrooms into the 'cultural islands' described, typically, in Hawkins. Through their efforts to reflect the relevant foreign cultures, they create an ambience evocative of sights worth seeing and many things worth smelling, touching, tasting, hearing and experiencing in neighbouring European lands. Our subject classrooms are carefully tended and kept fresh and stimulating, to a greater degree often, I believe, than many other subject classrooms. In addition to all of this we stage opportunities for our learners to encounter native speakers from these countries, either on our visits outward or on their visits to us. In the meantime, current technological developments in schools (particularly in the growing number of schools which are classed as language or technology colleges) are beginning to offer us a 'virtual reality' of our target language cultures. Thus it is clear that much is being done to open up a broader experience for our youngsters in a subject which is uniquely characterised.

However, this huge effort still falls seriously short of the kind of provision which would equate with that accompanying the L1, which enjoys the benefits of

The place and role of 'grammar' in the explicit/implicit debate — 11

'whole' conditions permitting 'immersion', conducive to the process of natural language absorption. In comparison, the L2 is negotiated in an enclosed setting, managed by one teacher who, however clever an exponent of the subject, is rarely a native speaker whose background and personal development had their sources in the pertinent foreign culture. Furthermore, not all schools continue to afford the employment of a Foreign Language Assistant in these times of budget difficulties. Add to these disadvantages the usually small time provision allocated to MFL study – the NC might have improved our case by pushing for more generous rates! – and the problem of serving this subject adequately, not to say well, increases ...

If we are now to leave the old teaching and learning patterns behind, (which permitted explicit classroom business, involving taking direct short cuts to information and knowledge), and replace these with techniques which mimic naturalistic L1 teaching (encouraging learners' foreign language **acquisition** as a result of a **'complete' experience** of it), then the time allocations we have for our purposes only mock the principle and our efforts to activate it! Acquisition needs time as our learners themselves demonstrate, having taken the number of the years in their ages to acquire their still relatively immature and imperfect competence in the L1. The simplest symbols describe the fragile position of foreign language pursuit in the experience of the average learner, as the following sketches show:

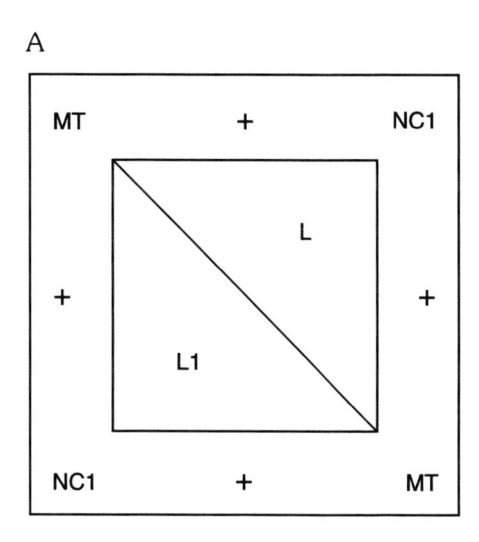

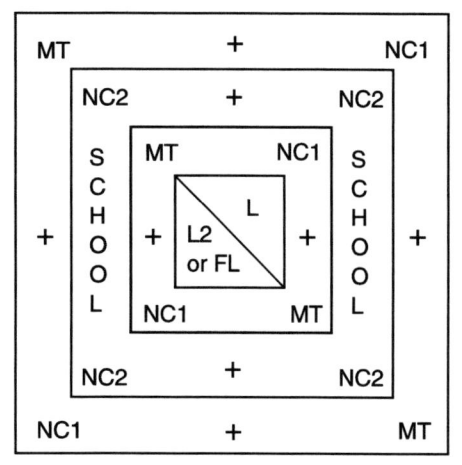

A

MT	+	NC1
+	L / L1	+
NC1	+	MT

B

MT	+	NC1
NC2	+	NC2
+	SCHOOL + [MT / L2 or FL / L / NC1 / MT] + SCHOOL	+
NC2	+	NC2
NC1	+	MT

L = Learner
L1 = first language
       ↓
MT = mother tongue
NC1 = native culture setting

L = Learner
L2 = second language
FL = foreign language
NC2 = National Curriculum
MT   NC1 as in sketch A

12 — REFLECTIONS ON GRAMMAR-IMPLICIT LANGUAGE TEACHING

The sections which now follow examine some of the similarities and differences which emerge in L1 and L2 (or FL) development.

SIMILARITIES AND DIFFERENCES IN L1 AND L2 DEVELOPMENT

(a) *Similarities*

- the existence of a 'tabula rasa': the argument that the learner starts from fresh;
- the need to train the hearing function as the primary function;
- the need to develop the mental processing ability;
- the need to collect vocabulary, expression, idiom;
- the need to fortify through use and practice the four language skills of Listening, Reading, Speaking and Writing;
- the need for explicit grammar teaching and learning to upgrade and improve development (in both L1 and L2) **once the learner has reached a point, at circa age 16, when there is the need for original, more complex language production.**

(b) *Differences*

- the degrees of immersion in the respective languages;
- the different contact frequency;
- the different perceptions of exposure to language and especially to prototype or adults' language as role-models' language;
- the ability to rely upon peer language in L1 and the lack of opportunity for this in L2;
- the environmental setting: natural and long term or artificial and short term;
- the presence of adults in large numbers and social variety in the L1 settings; the absence of adults in numbers and range in the L2 setting;
- the cultural and non-cultural contexts;
- the presence or absence of desirability, need, value, function, use, etc of the language and therefore of the sense of motivation and self confidence needed in order to pursue and master it;

- the different degrees of application possible for real(istic) everyday purposes;
- the question of the L1's application in real life as opposed to the L2's use in constructed scenarios for examination purposes or, at the average best, for reasons of short-term holiday survival;
- the learners' perception of each language: to be understood as a reality or as a myth;
- the different conditions of the language classes. In their English classrooms, learners use their already externally acquired competence as the tool for their performance. By contrast, in the foreign language classroom they have (for the most part) only the opportunities offered in their lessons on which to build the levels of competence which will allow them to perform.

The above lists of points are only representative of the many similarities and differences which characterise the L1 and the L2 or FL teaching and learning processes.

Some arguments in support of the use of naturalistic teaching styles in relation to L2

It would seem from the foregoing argument that, there being an arguably greater proportion of differences to similarities between L1 and L2 development systems, they would be better left different and addressed differently. Strangely, however, in writers' discussions the two are often brought together in support of a motion for the application of the L2 by naturalistic teaching and learning styles, of the kind which feature with regard to the L1. Some of the points given in MFL literature in support of this case are as follows:

- The means of language acquisition have been mastered by the L1 learner who, therefore, can apply these techniques to L2.
- Language, as we use it and teach it, is regarded as an entity, a 'Gestalt', the infinite potential of which is enabled by a small and definitive system of rules. Thus the larger concept should be given the priority in terms of focus and attention, and the smaller concept, the 'grammar', should be given its place in relation to the whole. It should not be taken out of context and treated out of perspective and disproportionately, and certainly not per se.

14 — REFLECTIONS ON GRAMMAR-IMPLICIT LANGUAGE TEACHING

- 'Consciousness raising' (as in Sharwood Smith 1981) is a more natural way than grammar instruction of enlightening learners of a foreign language to an awareness of that language, to a feeling about its structure and style and to the gradations of language management relevant to learners' age and linguistic development.

- Psychology should be used to generate and increase **motivation** levels in learners of the L2 or FL, even more urgently than in other subjects. This is argued on the basis of the perceived remoteness and lack of actual relevance to learners' lives that this curriculum subject has. From their training days teachers can recall their reading on the hierarchy of needs which includes **esteem for others** and **esteem for self**. In the classroom there would be much benefit to be derived from reciprocal **positive regard** and the encouragement of the learners' **self confidence**.

- Wilga Rivers (1983), already referenced earlier on account of her thinking on naturalistic methods of teaching and learning the FL, suggests that only the **reasonable** and **realistic** and **possible** and **sensible** and **relevant** should be taught. This is a simple condition which the 'grammar-translation' methods have not always applied. Indeed they have often over-indulged in contrived, highly artificial, inept and irrelevant matter.

- However, Rivers confirms language as rule-governed behaviour. This implies that the rules (the grammar structures) must be addressed and assimilated. She identifies two grammars: (i) the **pedagogical grammar**, that which is taught as building blocks, explicitly, as a grammar-for-grammar's sake agenda and (ii) the **linguistical grammar**, which is carried on the language, as an integral part of it, and is inseparable from it. Clearly this grammar also includes the pedagogical grammar, which is raised to consciousness, through 'implicit' teaching-tactics, rather than being abstracted, explicitly taught and possibly left disembodied.

- Krashen, influential in the 1980s with his views on L2 acquisition, advises that grammar, which has been taught to the learner explicitly, is not typically carried forward and applied. Rather it is used at the time of its introduction in exercises which practise its point discretely, before falling, out of context and detached, into disuse in the learner's mind. So, this implies that too much explicit grammar teaching can be a waste of time in the search to promote a language learner's levels of ability (at the stage of study which concerns us here).

Through naturalistic methods of teaching and learning, the youngsters' competence and performance levels can be addressed and fortified and the language being taught remains as a 'Gestalt'. This would not be the case with explicit grammar teaching, it is argued, which offers a fragmentary experience to the paradigm learners and to those who rely on the learning of set phrases and the technique of analogy-making as their means of generating foreign language. The writers, who have informed this section, formed and expressed their ideas on a holistic approach to L2 acquisition in the 1980s. The preparations for the NC for modern languages were apparent during the later 1980s leading to the initial Proposal of 1990. This made it clear that the influences behind the NC also had **acquisition** in mind for MFL classroom practice of the present and the foreseeable future.

For the purposes of the GCSE, the average learners will be conditioned to cope with their syllabus by the methods of its delivery. The above-average and talented learners, however, will be more ambitious in their coping attitudes, for they will require to use their FL more creatively and will therefore seek to free themselves from the constraints of the survival patterns. Thus they must internalise the grammar structures by engaging actively with them as they are floated on the classroom TL talk. **Simply, they must go to meet them, identify them and process them**. One remembers Chomsky on 'Universal Grammar' (UG) and 'Transformational-Generative Grammar' (TG), the persuasion that the human being is by nature programmed for language (UG) and can generate complex language of his own (TG). Many language teachers have encountered the influence of Halliday and Rivers, among others, but are particularly aware, perhaps, of Krashen's language users' 'editor' and 'monitor' mechanisms. These direct learners' powers of conscious learning, upgrading their levels of 'competence' to the benefit of their 'performance' and the quality of their creative output. Krashen's words, cited below, effectively summarise the writers' perspective on the desirability of applying the acquisitional development techniques, associated with the L1, to L2 (or FL) teaching and learning:

> '... second language teaching should focus on encouraging acquisition, on providing input that stimulates the subconscious language acquisition potential all humans have.' (1982, p.83)

Explicit (G-E) and implicit (G-I) procedures

The table which follows (page 16) separates the 'explicit' and 'implicit' language teaching procedures and allows the implications for the learners to be understood.

Accordingly, at this point a word from McArthur (1983) comes to mind. In considering and debating methodological issues in foreign language teaching, it is important to remember the responsibility on the part of teachers to make effective use of their methods and personal teaching styles, for they are in a position to exert considerable power and influence over the learners in their classrooms. This is the power to build or destroy. Clearly it is desired that teachers inspire, motivate, persuade, enable, empower their learners to engage with their brief in a responsible and enthusiastic way, finding satisfaction in the process and success in the end product, as their reward. The disaffected, undermined, diffident learners will not do the job that they are in the classroom to do. It will appear

THE EXPLICIT MODE (G-E) grammar is abstracted, formal, structured, sequenced, prescribed	THE IMPLICIT MODE (G-I) grammar remains embedded, unsequenced (ad hoc), inferred
• grammar points are declared and treated explicitly via explanation and analysis • grammar points are exercised in examples and practice, e.g. paradigm learning • grammar points are embedded in sentences and texts in order to contextualise them • grammar points are applied to extending contexts, systematically • grammar points are taught as a graded agenda • grammar competence is tested and measured, systematically • the teacher has full control	• no grammar point is abstracted; practice and play exercises hold grammar embedded, therefore implicit • structures emerge to the learners through the principle of exposure • inherent patterns are perceived, internalised, imitated via analogy and reinvented or recycled • 'new' language gradually emerges with the acquired structures embedded • grammar structures are increasingly absorbed and applied as the general TL application is stepped up • communicative competence can be assessed; it is in place thanks to the presence of grammar in the learners' language • the teacher lets go; the learners take hold

much too difficult to them and they will lose self esteem. Meanwhile, the brief that the teachers deliver in their classrooms, in this case the NC brief for MFL at Key Stages 3 and 4, will be coloured, as observed above, by their own personalities and their individual interpretations of what that brief means. Two teachers' lessons, ostensibly taught by the same approach, will carry marked differences. The following quotation is a clear expression of this notion:

> 'Teaching is an art. As an art, much of it is idiosyncratic, a personal achievement of the teacher.' (McArthur 1983, p.82)

The place and role of 'grammar' in the explicit/implicit debate — 17

It is possibly precisely the teacher's personal 'uniqueness' which makes each teacher vulnerable and potentially susceptible to criticism in relation to learners' poorer performances. Teachers know how vital it is to understand their learners' attitudes and the processes by which they deal with their task. 'Sympathy' and 'empathy' are principal elements of our stock in trade, as well as our general acceptance of the fact that some learners cynically militate against the desired good order and positive working atmosphere of the classroom, to frustrate our work and our pupils' progress. However, it is the teachers who face the responsibility for disappointing course outcomes. If results are poor, the quality of the teaching which led to those results is open to question. We are grateful for writers' objective expressions of common sense which confirm that if learners do not engage with their task, for whatever reason, no amount of teaching can establish their learning and secure their objectives for them. The teacher and the teacher's informed effort can provide only the spur to the learner's endeavour and subsequent attainment. Good psychology, the will to proceed positively to target, and trusting relationships must all be in place in a productive classroom, not least in NC times. **The learners must take responsibility for their learning** and accept the discomfort that this may cause them at times.

The German writer Schräder Naef (1978) represents the timeless advice offered typically by educational psychologists on a sensible and constructive, indeed essential approach for learners in relation to their targets. Learners' responsibilities and entitlements include the following:

- they must be able to make sense of their agenda;
- they must be motivated from within and from without;
- they must appreciate the learning for its own sake and value as well as for examination purposes;
- they must fortify their powers of concentration;
- they must avoid distractions;
- they must listen and focus;
- they must accept that they are responsible for their own learning (and not unjustly blame a poor end-result on alleged bad teaching);
- they must work in a way which facilitates proper completion of task;
- they must keep a balanced and positive outlook;
- they must be allowed to witness their progress happening;
- they must receive praise for their efforts.

So, while ideally we have our learners suitably primed for their task, we may take encouragement from the literature surrounding MFL practice, in order to proceed with our brief. This has been established as: L2/FL teaching by L1-related 'naturalistic' methods, featuring the G-I approach and all-purpose target language use. Each of the following selected quotations has a bearing on the matters of methodology that have been discussed in this chapter so far:

18 — REFLECTIONS ON GRAMMAR-IMPLICIT LANGUAGE TEACHING

> 'A (learner's) competency is more likely to develop from exposure than from instruction. And yet all instruction involves exposure.' (Ellis 1984, p.211)

> 'A teacher's view of grammar is crucial to how he or she will teach.' (McArthur 1983 p.103)

> 'If a teacher uses grammar, then it can either appear only in the books chosen and the work done, or it can be fitted in implicitly in the gradation of material that superficially appears to be grammar-free.' (ibid, p.104)

> 'The more we expect the learners to take in pattern indirectly, the greater the need for exposure to that pattern in use.' (Halliwell 1993, p.15)

> 'We do not set out to learn our mother tongue. We pick it up as we go along, through exposure to it and through the need to use it.' (ibid, p.16)

A recurring thought: one thing that has been lacking in FL teaching in recent times, say from the late 1960s increasingly, is the device of helpful cross-referencing from L2 to L1. Learners have come to know less and less about the composition of their native language, so that the provision of L1 grammar explanation has fallen into relative disuse in many establishments. At the time of writing this book (1997/98) we are told that the next decade will bring a turn around to this situation (e.g. *TES Extra*, English, 19 September 1997), since grammar teaching, so long described as useless, will return and be re-instated in classroom teaching as an **appropriate** content to be taught by **appropriate** methods at an **appropriate** age (derived from *Language is Power*, Honey J, 1997). Whatever happens with English, it will certainly have implications for the second and further foreign languages, as time will tell.

ANTICIPATING METHODOLOGICAL DEVELOPMENTS IN FL

Having reflected on the old and the new FL teaching approaches prior to examining, in action, the new, it will be interesting to observe generally whether we who teach foreign languages will succeed in making the NC preferred methods our universal standard policy for classroom use. Certain questions hang in the air, awaiting answers:

- Will these methods prove more effective, therefore more successful in terms of results?

- Will they generate increased satisfaction/enjoyment for learners?

- Will learners become better motivated, more positive and self confident?

- Will FL classrooms become happier arenas for learners to work in, on a subject which they will eventually come to value more highly?
- Will teachers show that they have the ability and the commitment to move to (and with) this prescribed NC policy for MFL?

My own study of two contrasting grammar teaching approaches and their effects on learners is described in the next chapters. Though it is an isolated experiment performed in a local setting, it will be seen to throw light on the following methodological strategies:

(i) the application of the G-I principle in relation to TL use and its implications for the teaching;

(ii) the annexing of the factor X (in the form of L1 grammar summaries) to G-I, creating my NC version of G-E, and the implications of this for the teaching;

(iii) the effects of these methods on the learners' subject-related attitudes and learning outcomes.

At the very least, there is the hope that our FL enterprise may be seen to have moved away from the sad attitude expressed, one might say, on behalf of too many others by a pre-NC Year 10 learner in the *cri-de-cœur* contained in the following poem:

Poème
'Je déteste'

Je déteste le français
Les mots!
Les verbes!
Surtout la grammaire!
Je déteste les heures dans
la salle de classe!
Le professeur!
Ma mauvaise humeur!
Je déteste le travail
La futilité
Les devoirs le soir
Les notes, les critiques ...
Je déteste le français!

Chapter 3

The action research (AR) plan

My plan to mobilise, in my FL department, an action research as a three-year foreign language GCSE course (French) was addressed through the application of the advocated NC teaching methods. This entailed organisation and planning at a number of levels, some of which are listed below:

- defining the grammar teaching principle; agreeing it and pledging to it;

- cohering, co-ordinating and harmonising our approaches to the AR project as a whole department, recognising identical responsibilities and accountabilities in addressing an identical task through a similar input, with generous rewards of experience potentially available for all;

- appraising each class of learners individually in respect of the ability status which it represented, therefore its learners' needs, strengths and weaknesses, and speculating on the realistically optimum targets they would be deemed capable of achieving in normal circumstances by eclectic methods; resolving to realise at least those targets in the AR;

- establishing the scheme of work or syllabus with its inherent grammatical agenda to be delivered in the main discreetly; matching this with a suitable programme of assessment;

- deciding the timetables and the time-scales which would structure the delivery of the syllabus and the assessment-plan;

- discussing and rehearsing the application of the agreed grammar teaching methods; exemplifying them;

- determining the teaching materials and some exercises and practices for common use;

- planning a number of lessons for individual or common application in order to accustom and harmonise teachers in their perception and practice of the selected (grammar-) teaching mode;

- structuring a system of meetings with teaching colleagues, for the purposes of focused discussion, feedback and constant updating of the work;

- agreeing the plans made by myself for using case-studies, recordings and questionnaires to access the learners' minds and uncover their attitudes, approaches and responses to their learning.

Preparing to activate the grammar-teaching principle

The NC documentation for foreign languages, specifically the Proposal of October 1990 (which echoes still in subsequent documentation), promoted a method of teaching from which sprang my own idea for two teaching styles for use in a contrastive study of grammar delivery. These were:

(1) an 'active' teaching style in which the FL grammar remains discreet, i.e. implicit, and is acquired by the learner through the target language experience, inferentially; and

(2) the same style to which, however, the teacher on occasions 'disembeds' the grammar that has, in fact, been the pedagogical agenda and explains it in the form of discrete items of grammatical summary expressed in English.

Appearing on the one hand to favour the first of these approaches, the document has expressed, on the other hand, some doubt as to whether the second is at all necessary, let alone desirable, as an extension of the teaching. Grammar summary is not deemed by the NC to imply any measurable benefit to learners' understanding and management of the foreign language and to their successful performance in it. However, the NC proposal offered no evidence or reasoning in substantiation of its statements on teaching method. Finding myself duly provoked, I responded by organising an action research designed to test the NC's methodological assumptions and staged it over three years in my departmental work place.

The first teaching style became my standard method, which I called M. In the contrastive exercise, involving two teaching approaches that I organised, this was common to both. Conducted exclusively in the target language (TL), it allowed no L1 interruptions of any kind and certainly none for grammatical or lexical explanation. Indeed, favouring no direct (explicit) grammatical exposé at all, it was designated, therefore, 'grammar-implicit' (G-I). It was used in its pure sense as M1. The counter-principle was an adaptation of M. When M was extended to include the factor X, it became M+X, therefore M2. The factor X was grammar-summary: explicit, descriptive and **retrospective** formal summary of grammatical content, delivered in the L1 with L1 written notes. This was the only context in which the L1 was to be used in the AR. It transformed M (M1) into M2 and facilitated my contrastive study of teaching strategies with particular emphasis on the grammar-implicit principle in which the NC invested its confidence for the new era in MFL teaching. Directly challenging those first statements made by the NC, I was deliberately questioning the efficacy of the grammar-implicit (G-I) approach as a stand-alone concept. I did this by testing the value of explicit grammar summaries delivered in English when these were used as a clarification device in FL work which had been conducted naturalistically by G-I.

Our arrangements for the teaching of French to GCSE, featuring the Year 9 intake of 1991, were established on a **split timetable** involving **parallel subject settings** as follows:

Side A of Year 9 Method M1 (G-I)	Staff	Staff	Side B of Year 9 Method M2 (G-E)
Set 'One' French 100 minutes per week	Myself	Myself	Set 'One' French 100 minutes per week
Set 'Two' French 125 minutes per week	Colleague 1a	Colleague 1b	Set 'Two' French 125 minutes per week
Set 'Four' French 50 minutes per week	Myself	Myself	Set 'Four' French 50 minutes per week

One or two points of explanation are required in relation to the diagram above:

- I ensured that I could be timetabled with the parallel Sets One and Four for the AR purposes. As the instigator and author of the methodological experiment, I was by definition the keenest, most accountable and most committed member of the team and would probably be the one who would remain with the AR and see it through, whatever conditions and circumstances might conspire against it over time. (This, indeed, turned out to be the case, and I was glad to be taking my turn with the two top sets! This was despite the fact that they lost one of their three weekly MFL lessons to German, at the expense of French, therefore.)

- Neither of the colleagues 1a and 1b could be timetabled with parallel sets as I was with the Sets One and Four. Accordingly, they worked in co-ordination with each other, negotiating their individual choices of M1 and M2 to suit their mutually perceived relevant aptitudes.

- The listed sequence of classes omits a Set 'Three'. This was due to the agreement that the colleague who would have been responsible for them would withhold her participation in the method trials. For this reason the middle sets, ie Sets Two and Three were mixed and shared out. This ensured that the abstaining colleague picked up two parallel classes as also did the participating colleagues 1a and 1b. By these measures I ensured that the AR was populated by a true cross-section of the Year 9 ability range.

- German teaching features typically for our top sets in Year 9. It was, accordingly, involved in the early stages of the AR but became redundant to its purposes later, when the two parallel Sets One German contracted into a single set for the pursuit of the GCSE in Years 10 and 11. The contrastive dimension of the method study was disabled in this instance. Since the study was discontinued for German post-Year 9, I do not include it for commentary in this account with the exception that I do allude briefly to the test performances of the Year 9 Germanists in the final analysis.

- The same lack of continuity, suffered in the German context, featured also with regard to my own Sets Four doing French. Even so, I will make brief mention of their performance with the methods applied to them in the coming chapters' discussion. Since they were learning French in common with the other AR sets, their contribution remains, to a certain degree, germane to this study.

THE MECHANISMS USED FOR ESTABLISHING THE SETTINGS

I turned to the Middle Schools' recommendations and learners' profiles as the means to inform my setting arrangements in the light of the learners' recorded abilities and aptitudes in the subject. I checked out my finished lists with those established by the other principal academic departments on the evidence of early Key Stage Sats results. We agreed to bring them into alignment as much as was reasonable and appropriate.

In particular the 'top' sets posed the problem. It was important to determine the top set calibre and to have the two top sets across the timetable divide well matched for the comparative exercise which awaited them. The 'bottom' sets (the Sets 'Four') were decided by the school's then Special Needs Organiser, so that these settings were defined and handed on to all subject departments as ready-made groups of matching traits and capacities. Once the top and bottom sets were established, the middle sets would be decided from the remaining pupils. (I have already explained how these were divided, without streaming, to form Sets Two and Three.) Finally, we felt confident enough to proceed with our structure and the action research.

However, the calibre of the year group as a whole presented us with a different concern. The informal and formal evidence which accompanied the intake's transfer from the Middle Schools and characterised the learners' performances in terms of attainment, aptitude and attitude, seemed to reveal this 1991 intake as one which might underachieve in general terms at school and so emerge untypical of its predecessors. The pupils came to us with this disappointing assessment and between the years 1991 and 1994 the school and the MFL unit found no reason to dispute it. However, there was no evidence of poor attitudes towards the school system itself and its expected standards of behaviour. My MFL colleagues and I shared a sense of optimism as we anticipated animating our designed three-year AR remit, featuring this year group and their French course to GCSE.

The agenda, materials and strategies used for teaching GCSE French by the selected (NC) methods

AGENDA

The major brief of the department was to teach French to GCSE for examination with the NEAB in 1994. This required us to apply to our task the last three years of a five-year agenda begun in the Middle Schools. The pyramid had a history of using the *Tricolore* course and associated publications, of which the Middle Schools used Stages 1 and 2 and the High School used Stages 3, 4A and 4B. The more advanced stages of the *Tricolore* GCSE course, structuring the High School's agenda, concentrated principally on **verbs and tenses** with a scattering of diverse other matters. We retained *Tricolore's* management and sequencing of this content for our AR purposes in order to lend common ground and a common frame of reference to our work. This was despite the fact that the NC disliked the notion of graded grammar teaching. However, in any co-ordinated exercise in which comparisons will be drawn there simply has to be a starting point, a system and a structure. (These must exist arguably also for the acquisition of the L1.) Then, full TL use would mix and merge all the aspects into a flow of language. The year-for-year scheme may be outlined as shown on p.25.

MATERIALS

The coursebook as 'materials'

In the first place, we had no option but to employ the *Tricolore* course, since this is what we had in stock. As has been seen, it linked our learners with their pre-High School subject pursuit, by agreement. It was not entirely suited to the NC intention for foreign language delivery, having a structure which contained explicit grammar features and end-of-unit summaries. *Tricolore* (in the version of the time) was and is, therefore, pro-grammar in essence, a compromise structural/communicative course, a ground-breaker at the time of its being marketed in the early 1980s. Thematically and topically, it represented the French culture and civilisation well. Also it provided rich practice for the language disciplines. However, its discrete grammar-features in English brought it out of sympathy with the NC's essential methodological ideal, G-I (although it supported perfectly the principle of L1 grammar summary in G-E as M2). Despite this difficulty there was no question of our suddenly buying a new choice of textbook for two reasons:

(i) We did not have the funds to do this.

(ii) Pro-NC course books were still being processed by their writers or in the publishing houses.

	Year 9: *Tricolore 3*		Year 10: *Tricolore 4A*		Year 11: *Tricolore 4B*
Unit 1	• the PERFECT TENSE • the VERB *devoir* (Present Tense) • the NEGATIVES	Unit 1	• Forming QUESTIONS (several ways) • ADJECTIVAL AGREEMENTS	Unit 6	• *jouer à; jouer de* • COMPARATIVES; SUPERLATIVES • EMPHATIC PRONOUNS • revision of PAST TENSES
Unit 2	• the FUTURE TENSE • consolidation of the PERFECT AND PRESENT TENSES, so that TIME becomes a concept	Unit 2	• the PERFECT TENSE (revised and extended)	Unit 7	• the use of REFLEXIVE VERBS • *en* + PRESENT PARTICIPLE • REPORTED SPEECH + *QUE* • RELATIVE PRONOUNS: *qui, que, dont* • INTERROGATIVE ADJECTIVES: *quel, quelle*, etc. • INTERROGATIVE PRONOUNS: *lequel, laquelle*, etc.
Unit 3	• revision of the complete PERFECT TENSE • revision of the complete FUTURE TENSE • revision of the PRESENT TENSE • consolidation of tenses for TIME discrimination	Unit 3	• the IMPERFECT TENSE (revised and extended) • CONCEPT OF TIME consolidated via revision of all the 4 major tenses	Unit 8	• DEMONSTRATIVE ADJECTIVES: *ce, cet, cette, ces* (inc. *-ci; -là*) • DEMONSTRATIVE PRONOUNS: *celui, celle, ceux, celles* (inc. *-ci, -là*) • revision of the INTERROGATIVE • the POSSESSIVE ADJECTIVES: *mon, ma, mes*, etc. • the PLUPERFECT TENSE
Unit 4	• PRONOUN OBJECTS, DIRECT and INDIRECT • POSITION AND SEQUENCE OF PRONOUNS • ADJECTIVES (a casual re-visit)	Unit 4	• FUTURE TENSE (revised and extended) • more on the REFLEXIVE VERBS	Unit 9	• VERBS separated by *à* or *de* • the CONDITIONAL TENSE
Unit 5	• the IMPERFECT TENSE • the IMPERFECT and the PERFECT, used in tandem • REVISION and CONSOLIDATION of the major tenses encountered so far • ADJECTIVES and AGREEMENT • RELATIVE PRONOUNS: *qui, que*	Unit 5	• *VENIR DE* + INFINITIVE • *ALLER* + INFINITIVE (immediate past and future) • DIRECT and INDIRECT OBJECT PRONOUNS and WORD ORDER (revised)	Unit 10	REVISION OF ALL GCSE GRAMMAR

In a way, my colleagues and I were not too unhappy in keeping our familiar textbook course as our main (though by no means only) teaching prop for the AR. Since we were due to take on a serious methodological challenge, we were happy to be on well trodden ground with our known textbook course. Our intention was to apply the coursebooks as they were for M2 (G-E). However, for our teaching by M1 (G-I), we would strategically disguise and by-pass the explicit areas. We recognised that inquisitive G-I learners, who took responsibility for their own progress and attainment, would explore the course as it presented itself and make themselves familiar with the textbook contents. This, however, was always the good learners' prerogative. If they did not have a textbook that explained matters to them, they could/would find one that did. However, we considered that it is more a matter of what **the teacher** prescribes and does in the classroom with the learners which decides **what** they learn and **how** they learn it. We were ready to observe to what degree this L1 explicit textbook feature tended to disrupt the G-I intention of our project and take measures accordingly.

An additional advantage of the *Tricolore* course was the **assessment system** that applied to it. This tested and appraised our learners' performances in the four language disciplines and provided a marks-to-points-to-grades performance summary which itself implied a forecast of an ultimate GCSE outcome, based on progress. The full range of assessment materials was used in tandem with GCSE/NEAB past examination papers. These vital mechanisms were applied at course unit completion stages and at key examination points on the school's 'internal' calendar, not least the 'Mocks'. Thus learners were kept conscious of their developments as GCSE linguists over the three crucial High School years and I, too, had a sound structure by which to take systematic measurement for my own AR purposes: (i) of the learners' MFL performance and (ii) of their comprehension and application of the FL grammar. There will be more on the outcomes of the measurement processes at a later juncture, however.

Miscellaneous materials

As well as by the formal, structured resourcing procedures discussed above, we further supported our lessons during the AR through the use of a variety of booklets and work sheets, some of them commercial and others home-made. Publications like *French in the news*; *French for comprehension*; *J'apprends à écrire*; *J'apprends à lire*; Mary Glasgow Publications' *Timesavers*; *French teacher absent* worksheets published by Cable Educational and further worksheet revision packs published by P and I Limited, as well as *Tricolore's* own activities-packs, gave us variety and flexibility. Even if a few of these gave their directions in English, these could be ignored and talked over in the L2. Certainly, they did not compromise the AR principle by presenting any of the foreign language grammar or through their use of the L1.

Our principal resource, however, was necessarily the teachers themselves with their own creative input of materials but also, and crucially, as talking heads. This is because of the single most important imperative of the NC methods being addressed, namely **the sustained and all-purpose use of the target language and the exposure of each class to this target language experience.** We knew before we started, that, under full TL conditions, the teacher would bring the grammar undeclared to her classes for, as has earlier been implied and is reasoned again here, the grammar, as an integral part of a language and its building blocks, floats with the language, is inseparable from it and cannot be ignored. A language carries and demonstrates its own grammatical, syntactical and lexical syllabus!

STRATEGIES

I intend in the next chapter to provide a number of extracts from transcriptions of recorded lessons which were delivered by methods M1 and M2 in the AR. Therefore I prefer for the moment simply to consolidate on the principal strategies which were employed for the purpose of conveying the grammatical agenda in a way that satisfied M (at the base of M1 and M2), remembering that the target language was required to articulate these strategies unfailingly. The following were the methodological 'staples' which we all agreed we could use:

- sentences around the class in turn-taking mode; the teacher uses sentences to exploit grammar-parts; similar others are invented by the learners through **inference** and **analogy**;

- a variety of exercises from the coursebook, or from the miscellaneous resources, selected to suit M;

- games played by the pupils; fun strategies; activities with a strong visual and 'hands-on' appeal; action-based exercises; inventive, self-made activities like word/phrase/sentence puzzles and jigsaws; role-plays; bound or mounted stories and playlets; cooking sessions and (video) film making; poetry writing;

- time given to alternative classroom management: individual/independent study; resource-based study; peer tutoring; pair-work and group-work etc; individual- or pair- or group-exposé of theme using board and chalk, OHP; flip charts etc;

- variations of 'therapy' activities: multiple-choice exercises; open-ended/ closed or direct requirement exercises; gap-filling tasks; course-related materials (adverts, posters, book covers, music sleeves etc); teacher made materials; collected materials for discussion and trading in a Swap Shop; back to familiar elementary experiences of 'tell and show'; learner-made materials with descriptions of why? how? where? when? for whom? etc; materials in listening, reading, speaking, writing; materials of all kinds with in-built differentiation etc.

- use of accompanying non-verbal language: body and face expressions to complement and enhance teacher- (or pupil-) talk; strategies relating to all forms of communication for emphasising, empathising and cueing the matter being taught or the message being delivered;

- use of apposites, opposites, contrasts, analogies, similarities, related things etc;

- use of retrospective, formal grammar summary in the L1 for the G-E sets whose brief was to learn the FL by the M2.

Consolidating the principal essential constituents of teaching method

Agenda, materials and strategies for the delivery of the classroom business can be separate principles only in a discussion on how each one in itself was constituted and organised. In a methodological exercise targeting a teaching/ learning experience, however, they come together to provide the collective propulsion that is, indeed, the lesson. The discussions which follow this chapter will uncover aspects of the taught syllabus which responded well or badly to the materials and modes of delivery. These developments occurred as they did for a number of reasons which the AR teachers succeeded in articulating, or for reasons which went beyond their ability to comprehend. However, it will be seen that the aim to proffer the FL grammar in such a way as to have it assumed naturally as a self-understood agenda was not at all an easy one to effect. The teaching materials had to match, or be adapted to match, the nature and requirements of the grammar targeted for delivery, on the one hand. On the other hand, the teaching strategies had to emphasise the grammar so that the learners could not avoid encountering it, dealing with it, internalising it for use, then and later. Hence the grammatical agendas, though undeclared (except as factor X) were **deliberately** and **explicitly**, though **discreetly**, treated by the teachers but never intended for conscious recognition or **discrete**, i.e. '**disembodied**' treatment by the learners.

The overall **agenda** was prescribed to us by the GCSE course. The **materials** were partly dictated by circumstances, partly they appealed to our collective or individual sense of creativity. Collectively, we could combine to produce a pool of useful items for use. Individually, we were not equally inventive. Our sense of invention affected also our response to the issue of **strategies**. Collectively, we gained from the discussions which we shared on the matter of methods. Individually, however, we were not all as flexible, as imaginative, as personally resourceful, as expansive as each other and not always to the extent that seemed necessary. The AR brought us closer together as a working team and revealed much about each of us as a teacher. It unfolded our strengths and weaknesses and, because the three areas of agenda, materials and strategies really do make **method**, which puts a lesson into drive, we were confronted with our own individual teaching performances in honest profile. **We saw ourselves teaching in the mirror. We saw ourselves reflecting on our practice at**

the mirror's critical and sometimes cruel cutting edge! In imposed self-analysis we recognised, at the least, areas which reflected our habits of complacency or of short-cut taking and it became obvious that, in addressing the NC by M, those habits would have no place. We understood the **crucial relationship** which binds the agenda to the materials chosen for practising it and to the strategies employed for addressing it. There was folly in short-changing any one of these criteria at the expense of the other two!

Undeniably, teachers are also forever learners. There was never a clearer understanding of this fact than during our methodological path-finding exercise. We gained a number of important insights as a result of our experience and observations. These are given brief mention here and may feature again in discussion later:

(i) We were thankful that we were dealing with a **spiral curriculum**! In the course of the three years to GCSE we knew that if we appeared to fail or disappoint our grammatical agenda at the first attempt to teach it, we would certainly encounter it again – and probably yet again! A glance at the roster drawn up earlier (see p.25) will confirm that there are very few items, and arguably no vital or complicated ones, that are not repeated. This helped (as it invariably helps) both ourselves and our learners. Indeed, we have always known that **revisitation** assists learners in their search for understanding. For one thing, what they are not ready to understand at one visitation, they might be better disposed toward at another. For another thing, the intervals between visitations of agenda permit the mind to process the difficult matters, so that repeated encounters allow clarification to happen, experience to grow and knowledge to result. We closely watched this kind of learning develop, and it became clear that there are right times and wrong times for learning to be attempted. We observed also our own success in refining our teaching incrementally in the same spiral context. At another level, and in the cases of less difficult concepts, repetition resulted in familiarity for the learners and their eventual confident and almost automatic handling of items of language. Over the course of time our learners displayed more confidence in comprehending and using the FL and we teachers, especially myself, became aware that the TL was beginning to form and emerge, as the pieces were carried forward and bonded together.

(ii) It became very obvious that the learners' role in the teaching/learning partnership was beneficial to successful learning when it was required to be an active rather than a passive one. This meant firstly that, by definition of M, the learners advanced to meet the information (agenda) proffered by the teacher, understood it by inference and converted it into knowledge. However, before that ever could happen, they were obliged to move beyond the teacher's lesson management and **use** the materials in order to engage with the strategies in a 'hands-on' way. Often they created their own exercises and directed their own management of them, in independent terms, or in responsible pair and group situations. This 'letting go' principle became a vital feature of the classroom business. However, because of the vulnerable nature of the subject – not many GCSE learners have adequate levels of FL on which to build authoritative communication – the teachers' leadership, sometimes open, sometimes discreet, was crucial to the classroom plan. This, by the new NC definition, had to be seen to be subtler, less than obvious and decidedly less didactic. In particular the teacher's voice, the source of the vital foreign language input, which sought to provide for all purposes and attempted to surround the learners with the foreign language, had to be omni-present, omni-directional and all-encouraging of the learners. The latter themselves needed to participate in the communication and do the difficult thing: **talk**.

(iii) The best returns and the greatest satisfactions were experienced when all of the learners' faculties were appealed to: their abilities to hear; read; write; speak; sing; write poetry; draw and label; tell and write stories; make and act plays; enact described scenarios; take dictation; correct each others' work; audio-record or video-record each other at work; discuss critically each others' work; give OHP exposés of tasks; peer teach; invent games; play games (e.g. it takes a sound sense of grammar to ensure that the Chinese Whisper message is correctly passed on!).

A final word would sum up all of the above observations in anticipation of the imminent analysis of the AR reality. Namely, teachers recognised that in using M their pupils responded best to any, as it were, **tangible** structures but, importantly, to all **visual** input that was made. Indeed, in the learners' responses to questionnaires – which were asked of them at half-termly intervals over the three years of the AR – the learners themselves expressed their interest in and preference for the teaching to be conducted by predominantly visual means, confirming that this had reliable and immediate appeal for them and a long term effect.

I have reserved the chapters which now follow for discussion of selected elements of the AR: aspects of the teaching; extracts from the teachers' discussions as well as from learners' discussions and questionnaires; a synopsis of the learners' main results; statements on the ultimate outcome of the AR, etc – all such matters as they factually happened during the three years of the GCSE/AR which was carried out in my department from 1991 to 1994.

Chapter 4

Grammar-implicit (G-I) teaching in action

The grammatical agenda pursued on behalf of the 1991 Year 9 intake as representative of their syllabus content for the three years to GCSE has been itemised in the preceding chapter. I shall allude to its components as I now attempt to clarify the ways in which we tackled it by M, common to both M1 and M2. At times, I intend to describe also the conversion of M1 into M2 by adding the factor X component, using random examples to illustrate how we did this on a regular basis on behalf of the G-E classes in the experiment. My critical commentary on our performance as method deliverers in the context of the NC's advocation of the Method which I term M will be phased throughout this chapter and summarised in conclusion. With that established, I shall now proceed to concentrate on giving a selection of lesson descriptions from the range pertaining to the **Year 9 syllabus**. This restriction is due to the limitations of time, space and opportunity preventing me from extending the inquiry into the lessons held in M across the whole breadth of the three-year French course, which was often an iterative one anyway. More clarity will be derived if readers are able to refer to the course-book *Tricolore 3* at times.

The teaching programme in Year 9

French was used as the only medium of talk in the classrooms (except when English was employed in delivering the factor X). Thus the learners became accustomed to coping with the idea of all-purpose TL communication as a matter of policy. Clearly, at this early stage and for the duration of the course, they understood much more than they spoke. Although they interacted with the teacher in French, the collective voice of the class would not generate as much talk as the single voice of the teacher and the class members addressed each other sparingly in the FL. This is an observation which receives much comment from MFL writers and researchers in current times. Yet I am surprised that they are so easily critical of it. There is little – and only contrived! – opportunity for the practical FL development to take place, that one must feel gratified to witness it happening at all. By the very nature of the subject this must be the case, especially when one takes into account the persistent problems affecting class (and

32 — REFLECTIONS ON GRAMMAR-IMPLICIT LANGUAGE TEACHING

classroom) management, such as the syllabus demands, class sizes and time constraints.

What will now be discussed are the matters of pedagogical grammar which we applied for Year 9 purposes in the AR. These were still given a formal place in the GCSE syllabus at the time of the AR and received formal treatment in the coursebook used in that period. In the new methodological development, however, the pedagogical grammar is integral with the ubiquitous linguistical grammar and is demonstrated and practised through the TL application accordingly.

THE VERB *DEVOIR* IN ITS PRESENT TENSE
(with implications for any other present tense verb which is newly encountered and merits clarification)

Phase One

The teacher relied on the learners managing to understand, inferentially, her intentions in using the parts of *devoir*. She allowed a genuine incident to be the impetus for negotiating the grammar. This, indeed, had been her plan. A pupil came out to the front of the class and asked for early release from the lesson:

P1	*Puis-je aller à neuf heures et demie aujourd'hui, madame?*
T	*Pourquoi ça?*
P1	*Aller à la dentiste.*
T	*Oui, bien sûr. Bonne chance chez le dentiste!*
	(to the class) *Hélène doit aller chez le dentiste à neuf heures et demie. Alors, c'est nécessaire; elle est obligée. Tu as mal aux dents, oui?*
P1	*Oui, hier.*
T	*Dommage. Hélène doit aller chez le dentiste aujourd'hui. Qu'est-ce que tu dois faire aujourd'hui, Kirsty?*
P2	*Aller chez ma grand-mère.*
T	(prompts) *Je dois ...*
P2	(eventually) *Je dois ... aller chez ma grand-mère.*
T	*Pourquoi ça?*
P2	*Faire les courses. Elle est malade.*
T	(addressing the class) *Kirsty, qu'est-ce qu'elle doit faire?*
Ps	*Aller chez sa grand-mère ... Faire les courses ...*
T	(presses the class) *Elle ...*
Ps	*Elle ... doit faire les courses ...*
T	(addressing the class) *Vous autres. Vous devez aller chez vos grands-parents ...?* etc.

And so it continued across the conjugation until the teacher decided to refer to some relevant structured exercises in the textbook.

Phase Two

The teacher wrote the exercises on the blackboard. The references pertained to *Tricolore 3*, p.12:

(a) *Devant le lycée* and

(b) *Pour bien profiter d'un séjour à Paris.*

In terms of exercise (a) she said:

T	*Lisez le passage et notez les situations de nécessité. Soulignez-les de votre crayon. Moi, je vais écrire vos réponses au tableau noir, après.*

She did this, thus placing the parts of the verb *devoir* on the board as the pupils uncovered and declared them.

Exercise (b) asked the learner to take a number of random sentences and re-state them in order of importance. They all focused on *devoir*, each using one person of the verb and collectively covering the verb. By moving the sentences about (in an exercise which had no definitive solution) their familiarity with *devoir* was fortified. The teacher asked for suggestions to be written (by the learners) on the board. When some mistakenly wrote the wrong verb part, others reacted and were invited to come to the board and correct the mistake:

T	(reading the verb parts from the blackboard and pointing them out with the board ruler, went over the full exercise, the beginning of which was as follows):
T	*Moi, quand je veux voir Paris, je dois mettre des chaussures comfortables. Et toi, David? Qu'est-ce que tu dois faire?*
David	*Moi, quand je veux voir Paris, je dois prendre une semaine de congé.*
T	*Et toi, Kate?*
Kate	*Moi, quand je veux voir Paris, je dois aller à l'office de tourisme, pour demander un dépliant de la ville et un plan du métro.*
T	*Julie, qu'est-ce qu'elle doit faire, Kate?*
Julie	*Elle doit aller ...* etc.

NB The verb *devoir* in grammar-summary form

A formal spoken observation and a written note of explanation about the Present Tense conjugation and the use of the modal auxiliary verb *devoir* were given to the G-E class: The explanation extended to the juxtaposed verb in its infinitive form. Some of the exercises were run through again quickly, in order to illustrate the formal and metalinguistically styled comments.

THE NEGATIVES

The aim was to 'experience' the six most common expressions known at this level as 'the negatives' as indicated on page 26 of the coursebook *Tricolore 3*.

1. *ne ... pas* (not)
2. *ne ... plus* (no longer)
3. *ne ... jamais* (never)
4. *ne ... rien* (nothing)
5. *ne ... personne* (nobody)
6. *ne ... que* (only)

Of the above six matters, the pupils had brought some familiarity with the first one with them from their Middle Schools. Most of them remembered *pas* but relatively few were able to sandwich the verb between *ne* and *pas*. The teacher manufactured the need for a negative response and built up a framework for the use of the other negatives from there. The starting point might be a question like:

T	*Tu arrives en retard à la leçon, Hayley?*
Hayley	*Non, madame.*
T	*Mais tu arrives souvent en retard, je crois?*
Hayley	*Non, madame.*
T	(encouraging) *Non, madame, je ...*
Hayley	*Non, madame, je ... arrive pas en retard.*
T	*Non, madame, je n'arrive pas en retard* (emphasising *ne ... pas* with the voice).
	(then) *Hayley n'arrive jamais en retard* (emphasising with the voice).
T	*Ça, c'est une réponse au négatif. On peut dire: ne ... pas ou ne ... jamais. Aussi d'autres choses. Il y a d'autres négatifs comme vous allez découvrir en lisant les textes pour aujourd'hui:* Conversations. *Tournez à la page vingt-six.*

The conversations were read by the teacher with the pupils' apparent understanding. The teacher accompanied her reading with the following non-verbal communications:

- body and facial expressions;

- further examples of the same item for reinforcement;

- symbols on the blackboard like ✓ and ✗ or ☺ and ☹ to carry meaning corresponding to the text;

- descriptions as definitions or contradictions to carry forward the meaning intended.

For example, teaching *ne ... pas* and introducing *ne ... rien*:

Grammar-implicit teaching in action — 35

Qu:	Avez-vous vu le film sur Napoleon hier soir?	✓	Oui, j'ai vu le film	☺
		✗	Non, je n'ai pas vu le film	☹
Qu:	Avez-vous acheté beaucoup de choses à Paris?	✓	Oui, j'ai acheté beaucoup de choses à Paris	☺
		✗	Non, je n'ai pas acheté beaucoup de choses:	☹
			– pas de souvenirs	☹
			– pas de cadeaux	☹
			– pas une seule carte postale	☹
			– rien: absolument rien	☹
		✗	Non, je n'ai rien acheté	☹

Most of the negatives were dealt with in this way. Learners enjoyed this grammar which they perceived as a game with words. They convinced their teacher that, by the end of the lesson, they understood (a) the negative expressions and their meanings and (b) the split structure of the expressions and how to wrap them around the verb.

Some of these expressions were easier to learn than others: *ne ... pas* was familiar from the start; *ne ... jamais* was appealing to our learners; and *jamais* had a more 'solid' meaning, they said; *ne ... plus* was interchangeable with *seulement* which they understood as 'only'; *ne ... personne* was perhaps the most logical of all, because they understood *personne* as a positive and *ne* cancelled it out into 'no person', therefore 'nobody'. The next step was simply to go around the class in response to the teacher's stimuli:

T	Dites-moi quelque chose au négatif.

A lot of activity built up in relation to this grammar:

- going out of the classroom door at the end of the lesson, prior to break, to leave the room empty and therefore **nobody** is in it;
- handing in the homework as people who allegedly **never** forget it;
- passing with difficulty the teacher's handbag as something which is **not** or **never** empty or light;
- investigating the teacher's chalk-box which has **only** three sticks of chalk in it one moment and **nothing** in it the next.

The hands-on referencing of classroom paraphernalia – touching, feeling, handling, emptying, filling, etc – whilst causing laughter (and a certain nuisance factor also, admittedly) became an important aspect of the teaching approach and classroom routines. It also established itself as significant in the development of the process of association in the pupils' minds. The **visual** characteristic of the classroom agenda became the most important one. This clearly was the case in the teacher's perceptions and it was declared by the learners in discussions and questionnaires to be the case for them equally. For example, on the occasions when colour coding procedures were employed in blackboard, OHP or flipchart work, the colours which coded important grammatical factors for the purpose of emphasising them to the learners' minds then became permanently associated with those factors. In any case, the more visual the lessons were made the more effective, enjoyable and successful they were considered to be. The 'negatives' scarcely registered as a problem at all. The difficulty remained in the form of the verb that split them.

> **NB The G-E grammar: summary of 'the negatives'**
>
> Using the L1, the G-E pupils were required to write out the rubric located in their textbooks on p26: 'More about saying something that is not, never, no longer etc ....' The teacher emphasised the split structure of the item and the nature of the verb as the word which was surrounded. The exercises were revised in the light of the grammar. The text was explained orally and new examples were invented in French and discussed: *Le professeur n'a que deux cahiers; L'étudiant n'oublie pas son cahier; On ne prend pas le métro* etc. The textbook explanation clarifies further the difficulties of the negative of the perfect tense when the applied present tense parts of *avoir* or *être* are considered to be the working verb. The placing of the negative around the auxiliary proved to be a confusing item for the G-E learners, since they suddenly found themselves with something other than the negative, and more complicated than the negative, to consider explicitly. (Isn't the perfect tense invariably more complicated than most other things in the mind of the average learner?)

THE PERFECT TENSE

This massive grammar agenda is considered daunting by today's standards in grammar teaching and learning. It clearly dominated the French syllabus throughout the three years of study in that it was a ubiquitous part of the relevant spiral curriculum, receiving more serious treatment and attention than any of the other featured tenses (future, imperfect, conditional). In the external examinations at GCSE there are, now as then, expressed expectations that the perfect and future at least should be applied by learners who wish to establish their merit as Higher Level achievers. (The present tense remains the province of the Basic level, now Foundation Tier, candidate.) The spiral curriculum enables a number of (re)visitations of this agenda. The materials which articulate it and continuously feature it benefit the learners' assimilation of it and lighten the teacher's onus of delivering a critically difficult matter by subtle, i.e. less than analytical means. This is in any case an agenda which is structured on a number of levels. It lends itself to incremental and iterative teaching.

Beginning in Year 9, we used *Tricolore 3*, which was clear, thorough and not intimidating where the teaching of the perfect tense was concerned. The outlay of this agenda was going to be of great benefit to the G-E classes, once the matter had been treated by M. At the outset, we wondered about the factor of L1 intrusion. If the learners were to succumb to the temptation of mentally referencing the L1 in their search for a way to express a past action, we would make gain if their L1 example suggested the two-word form including part of 'to have' and a past participle. If, however, the L1 suggested a single word past tense for the activity in question, this would certainly confuse the youngsters. After these stages, the French would produce enough problems of its own with (a) irregular past participles; (b) verbs using the auxiliary *être* instead of *avoir*; (c) the difficult and irregular present tenses of *avoir* and *être* in themselves; (d) subject-related agreements of the past participles with verbs using *être*; (e) agreements of the past participles with verbs using *avoir* when these featured a preceding direct object.

Before we started our work on the perfect tense, we decided that the last of the above listed matters was, in fact, not going to be addressed at all. Not by M, and not as part of 'French for all'. It could easily wait to be taken up as part of French for the minority and be aired at Sixth Form level. So, it was by-passed with some relief on our part.

The action on the perfect tense

The management of this agenda was done

(a) casually, through initial conversation, discussion, using natural excuses for talk that emerged and time-locking them with expressions that relegated the action in question to the past: *hier; la semaine dernière; ce matin; hier soir; la dernière fois; il y a cinq minutes, deux semaines*, etc. This occurred at the simplest levels, e.g. on the teachers' checking in the pupils at registration and inquiring about their homework, whether it was done and ready for handing in or not. The dialogue started in the following way:

T	*Vous avez tous fait vos devoirs? Andrew, toi aussi? Tu as fait ton devoir? David, tu as écrit ton exercice?*
	Kirsty, tu m'as donné ton cahier?
	And so on.

(b) with respect to the exercises structured in the course book. At the current point of the practice this began with *Tricolore 3*, p.18 'Cartes postales de Paris'.

38 — REFLECTIONS ON GRAMMAR-IMPLICIT LANGUAGE TEACHING

Christine, during her visit to Paris, wrote five postcards. Some of the messages contained in each one told about things that she **has done**. Therefore they were communicated in the perfect tense with a number of them repeated several times. The result of this was typically that the pattern that they represented took a more certain hold in the learners' minds than would otherwise have been the case. This idea was repeatedly put into action;

(c) using cut-up sentences originating from designed then fragmented transparencies for use with the OHP. For example, the pupils were asked to reassemble the pieces that they saw jumbled on the screen so as to restore the original sentences and their meaning. Or they were given batches of materials in the form of jigsaws in order to do similar things with these. By working in pairs and small groups, they were able to discuss their efforts, gain from trading opinions and from drawing from some people's *savoir faire*. Such activities were generally greatly enjoyed. Further games and exercises of this ilk were developed and tried out, with a positive reception in the main.

Back to mode (b) for more detail on the coursebook support for this item. The course dealt with the French perfect tense in its two principal stages: (i) the perfect tense with *avoir*; (ii) the perfect tense with *être*. This discussion focused on examples of the perfect tense contained in each of Christine's five postcards, as shown below:

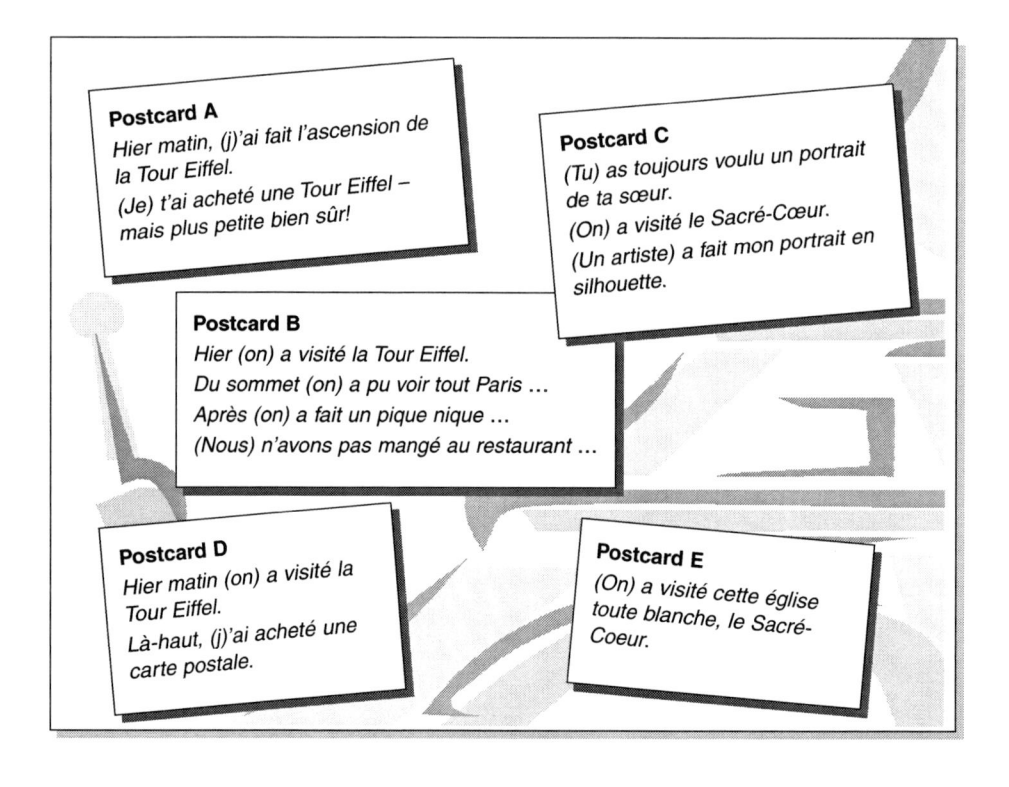

Postcard A
Hier matin, (j)'ai fait l'ascension de la Tour Eiffel.
(Je) t'ai acheté une Tour Eiffel – mais plus petite bien sûr!

Postcard C
(Tu) as toujours voulu un portrait de ta sœur.
(On) a visité le Sacré-Cœur.
(Un artiste) a fait mon portrait en silhouette.

Postcard B
Hier (on) a visité la Tour Eiffel.
Du sommet (on) a pu voir tout Paris ...
Après (on) a fait un pique nique ...
(Nous) n'avons pas mangé au restaurant ...

Postcard D
Hier matin (on) a visité la Tour Eiffel.
Là-haut, (j)'ai acheté une carte postale.

Postcard E
(On) a visité cette église toute blanche, le Sacré-Coeur.

Grammar-implicit teaching in action — 39

The teacher read each postcard carefully with the class before requiring individual pupils to read out postcards of their choice, allowing sufficient turns to be taken around the class to effect familiarity with the texts, encouraging the development of the right 'feel' for the sound – the 'hunch' factor. The teacher's next instruction was :

T	*Prenez un crayon maintenant et soulignez soigneusement les activités de Christine. Par exemple, moi, je commence par souligner l'expression de la première activité: hier matin j'ai fait l'ascension etc. Alors, continuons ... et complétons l'exercice à travers les cinq cartes postales.*

The pupils worked at underlining the perfect tense items in silence.

T	*Maintenant, vous allez me dire les exemples que vous avez trouvés et moi, je vais les écrire au tableau noir.*

The teacher made a clear list on the blackboard of the abstracted items and in so doing she placed in brackets alongside them the infinitives from which the past participles had been derived, in the following manner:

j'ai fait (faire)
je t'ai acheté (acheter)
nous n'avons pas mangé (manger)
on a visité (visiter)
tu as fini (finir) etc

Further symbols, brackets and colour-codings were used after that in order to identify the various traits of this difficult grammar concept. They initially focused, incrementally and selectively, on the perfect tense with *avoir*, hoping to be treading on familiar territory already encountered in Middle School Year 8 classrooms. In a conversation with the Middle Schools of the pyramid later, however, our relative understandings of the incremental syllabus became suddenly clearer. Indeed, Middle School colleagues pointed out that careful perfect tense planning in their context implies taking much shallower sections of the agenda for incremental and graded teaching. For example, they concentrate principally on the reliable and regular conjugation involving *avoir* and the 'er' verb. Clearly, the 14 to 18 High School teachers are unused to dealing with the younger learner, beginning the pre-GCSE course (Key Stage 3). Perhaps they expect of their learners too much, too directly, too soon? Certainly, on the issue of the perfect tense, speculation of this sort was very tempting.

Having said all of that, and having at the time in question delivered my own lessons on the perfect tense with *avoir* in the ways described above, it seemed to me that my pupils had experienced little difficulty with the agenda – **at least at the time of its delivery** – and had quite enjoyed it, indeed. Realising that the real difficulty with this grammar-episode lay in the matter of the irregular past participles, I instigated some drills in which those which mattered to our purpose were uncovered and practised. I ensured that the associated infinitive verbs were clearly spotlighted also by means of the assorted codings already alluded to. For those who are acquainted with *Tricolore 3*, such drill exercises as those used included the following:

- *Répondez* (p.18), a multichoice exercise aiming to impress the perfect tense pattern;

- *La Journée de Michel* (p.19), a more sophisticated multichoice feature which requires extended development of the verbs;

- a story board (p.19), expressing the activities of stick people in the perfect tense;

- two graded exercises of textual study (pp.20–21) in which the texts contain gaps to be completed by the learners in terms of their supplying correct and appropriate perfect tense verb parts.

NB The perfect tense grammar: summary

The formal, explicit teaching component which was administered to the G-E learners was given, as usual in the form of spoken and written summary of the perfect tense, in English. The stages of this consolidation were as follows:

1. the purposeful reading of the relevant grammar blocks (textbook pp.19, 21);

2. note-making from the information contained in the blocks;

3. the teacher's advice to the pupils to learn four things:
    - the principal rules of the perfect tense
    - the verbs *avoir* and (for future reference) *être* in the present tense;
    - the list of irregular past participles;
    - (a caveat for future consideration), the list of verbs taking *être* in the perfect. A comment explaining this extension of the perfect tense grammar was supplied;

4. overall discussion, reappraisal of the exercises in the light of this consolidation;

5. anticipating the further developments of this tense.

Note: All applications of the perfect tense with *être* – which had already occurred and would certainly feature frequently from then on – were assisted for the purposes of G-I by the use of story-board aids, involving the gamut of relevant verbs placed in a narrative sequence to appeal to the learner's memory. Rhyming devices also featured.

THE FUTURE TENSE

In my discussions with teachers of French, it is most often agreed that the future tense is a grammatical agenda which would seem to be well suited to the principle of G-I. I would concur with them and at the time of the AR I anticipated finding this to be the case as I and my colleagues set out to deal with it. The future-stem exceptions aside, there would seem to be no reason why this item should not be implicitly introduced, made familiar in association with its temporal adverbs, and absorbed as a well defined, well shaped, memorable tense for purposes of recognition, comprehension and use by our learners. However, we encountered from the outset some unexpected resistance which I was able to reflect on and rationalise as follows:

- Our approach to the future tense succeeded our treatment of the perfect in the sequenced grammar syllabus that we had adopted. The 'perfect' teaching had contained the difficulty of emphasising the use of two verb-words (the appropriate present tense part of *avoir* or *être* and the past participle), despite the fact that the learners, who, arguably, instinctively mentally accessed their L1 (English) knowledge to inform them on difficult matters such as this one, did not always emerge from that incursion with a word for word L1 counterpart. For example, they would very often be informed of a single word meaning when referencing the 'perfect' activity in English, e.g. 'I did' for 'I have done'; 'I went' for 'I have gone'. Therefore they would wish to supply a single word counterpart in French. This is not to mention, of course, further difficulties involving 'did and the infinitive'. Accordingly, a great deal of effort and persuasive, manipulative teaching was invested in the perfect tense in order to manage it successfully as a two-word-tense and make this pattern a reliable reality in the minds of the learners. (It must be remembered all along that, the learners' minds often computed **words** which furnished meaning, not necessarily **verbs**.) Then along came the future tense. At the teacher's first sight (in its pure form) it seemed very conveniently packaged in French as a one-word tense. However, there was much irony in this, since our learners, on cross-referencing with their L1, were informed of a two-word situation. For them a new frustration ensued, and for us a further challenge! My reflections at this point in my AR diary were as follows:

- MFL teachers are fully aware of the difficulties attendant in their teaching the one-word tenses in French, when the native language often uses two as standard practice. The three-way difficulty characterising the L1 perfect tense, as just mentioned, reflects also, consistently, the three-way route by which the L1 present tense itself is articulated: 'I go'; 'you are going'; 'he does go'. Whereas, the 'perfect' requires two-word elements in French, the French 'present' requires one. This has always been a matter of conspicuous difficulty for our average learners of French. It now featured again with the future, as we AR teachers strove to persuade them to absorb the English term 'will' and see the 'r' stem-ending and the range of special future endings as the French way of compensating for this clearly important omission made in the French one-word tense.

- Tense-work overall is a highly complex business, both in itself and in its relation to the cognitive development of our adolescent learners below the age of sixteen years. I recall that this was the case also in the grammar-translation days of the GCE, when the learners' whole conditioning was towards technical perfection based on grammatical precision.

It was a matter of some surprise and embarrassment to me that I stumbled in my first efforts to deliver the future by M. Hence my reflections, above, on the reasons why this should have happened. Patently, however, we were all of us – teachers and learners alike – already exhausted by our efforts to deal with the perfect tense. As a result, I found myself being very **explicit** with the future, although not in the manner of employing the L1 (except in its proper role as the factor X with my G-E classes). My colleagues 1a and 1b were in the same frame of mind as myself. Indeed colleague 1b, who had elected to apply M2 to her work, lost the reins of her method. She found herself teaching in a heavily compromised way, in which the L1 explanation, which should have been reserved as an end-of-component factor X, in fact interrupted and, as it were, dominated her agenda from start to finish. In her turn, colleague 1a, teaching by M1, restricted her teaching to very narrow lesson-plans based on coursebook matter and exercises. She relied on equally narrow rapid and sketchy future tense pattern-practice, done in the foreign language. However, she resisted the temptation to prejudice her G-I brief by using the L1 to assist clarification.

My own lessons featuring the future tense followed a similar pattern for all of my teaching sets, both the two Sets One and the two Sets Four. All of my lessons – for I found myself needing to go over the subject several times for all of the reasons outlined earlier – echoed the ideas used also by my colleagues 1a and 1b. Some sections of lesson-transcriptions have been abstracted as a means of illuminating our difficulty in executing this grammar agenda by the method M.

The steps of the first future tense lesson

1. Turning to page 40 of the textbook (*Tricolore* 3), the pupils were asked (in French) to underline or ring in pencil the words of action which featured in the reading text.

2. The teacher and class went through the examples, locating them by quoting line and word numbers as references.

3. Words appeared in the purview like:

    il a quinze ans; il habite à Paris ...
    il passera ses vacances à Saverne ...
    je partirai en Alsace, etc.

4. Of the 'action words' listed, the pupils were asked to group them as (a) action words with which they were familiar and (b) action words which were new to them.

5. Looking on the blackboard the teacher attempted to explain three time-aspects involving these action words as 'present', 'past' and 'future'. In order to do this she further demonstrated this explanation of time through the use of adverbial phrases like:

maintenant; en ce moment etc (present time)
hier; avant-hier; il y a une semaine etc (past time)
demain; après-demain; dans un mois etc (future time).

Examples of use were gradually extended in a way which demonstrated one verb and context and expanded into several verbs and contexts as follows:

aujourd'hui	je fais mes devoirs	je fais les achats pour maman	je travaille en classe
hier	j'ai fait mes devoirs	j'ai fait le jardinage pour papa	j'ai regardé la TV
demain	je ferai mes devoirs	je ferai une visite au cinéma	je sortirai en ville

6. The teacher referred back to the original coursebook exercise. It was read again with the verbs emphasised in context.

7. In the coursebook exercises the various separate verb parts were sought so that the complete conjugation came together. Each 'person' of the verb was made to stand out through pencil underlining in the text. On the blackboard, they were written up – apparently casually! – and colour-coded in three stages of emphasis applied to:
   (a) the temporal adverb;
   (b) the end-of-stem 'r';
   (c) the 'person'-related verb ending.

8. Further examples were exercised in relation to a range of temporal adverbs evoking the future tense use.

9. Examples were required of the pupils in turn-taking-mode, involving all of them, around the class.

10. A game was set up: question-and-answer based on the use of the future and the 'pick a victim' process which the teacher habitually used.

In the succeeding lesson the emphasis was put on creating a more expansive impression of the future. The influence of more advanced adverbial expressions like *demain; la semaine prochaine; dans un mois/deux ans*, etc was enlisted. All efforts to exemplify verbs in the future tense, however casually they were applied, concentrated on drawing the learners' attention to the verb-stem, ending in '*r*', and brought together all the verb parts, so that the full sequence or conjugation was demonstrated. Even the superfluous '*e*' of the '*re*' verbs was neatly disposed of through coding, in selected examples. Soon, pupils could easily recognise this tense, having quickly appreciated its distinguishing characteristics: the end-of-stem '*r*' and the endings based on *avoir*. Therefore they were prepared to infer meaning correctly in exercises of 'Listening' and 'Reading' comprehension when the message was related to future time. Before long they were able to attempt the use of the future tense in 'Speaking' and 'Writing'. Their work brought many good and imaginative examples to the fore. However, their incorrect attempts were interesting from the point of view of what they revealed of the potential for error in this concept. This in itself offered the teacher valuable insight into the learners' perceptions of the difficulties so that remedial L2 teaching could be followed up and partly conveyed on the process of discreet correction. Some typical examples follow:

- *Demain je visiter le cinema.* The pupil knew that this regular verb's infinitive must be used as the future stem, but could not proceed to 'step two'.

- *Demain nous écouteons la radio.* The absence of the future-stem '*r*' brought this example so near yet so far in relation to the solution sought!

- *Demain je travaillai dans la maison.* This is the example of a learner who could not juggle with two items at one time and let one drop: namely the '*er*' ending of the future verb-stem.

- *Demain je serai visiterai mon ami.* This example demonstrated the zeal of an enthusiastic very able learner who, however, had not remembered to reduce her L1 reference to one word. On accessing English for her example she continued to treat it in literal translation, but offered us two beautifully formed 'futures' in the process!

The best work on the future tense was yet to be done! We discovered that it was very well suited to (multi-purpose and generally very beneficial) tense-consolidation work in which we featured it in action with the 'present' and the 'perfect'. It was an easy matter to set up multiple choice exercises, for example, in which the correct tenses were determined by the associated time adverbs, e.g. *aujourd'hui*; *hier*; *demain* and others. Also story telling and scenario descriptions were developed to make sense of the tenses:

> *Ce que fait ma mère aujourd'hui ...*
> *Ce qu'a fait ma grand-mère il y a des années ...*
> *Ce que, moi, je ferai dans dix ans ...*

In this section I have attempted to demonstrate the future tense in the real terms of its rather problematic relationship with M. In the end, however, there was a general feeling that we were comfortable with it and had enjoyed our experience of it. We had, admittedly, used arguably 'explicit' inroads for delivering this agenda but we felt we would cope with it to our greater satisfaction in the terms of M, on encountering it on each further future occasion. Meanwhile, the G-E sets received their formal explicit summary in English.

It was interesting that the Sets Four registered enthusiasm for the work that they did in relation to the future tense. It was important for their performances in comprehensions that they could recognise it. And recognise it they did! The characteristics of the 'r' and the endings were quickly discerned and the time-sense of the future was rationalised in connection with the idea of 'soon' and in contrast to other time senses, like 'now' and 'then'. The Set Four learning by G-E or M2 was able to activate its own selected verb in the future tense. It correctly applied the future endings to the whole infinitive of *adorer*, used properly as the future stem and featuring the 'r'.

THE REMAINING YEAR 9 GRAMMAR SYLLABUS

The outstanding items still to be discussed are:
- nouns;
- adjectives;
- comparatives/superlatives;
- pronouns (direct object and indirect object);
- the imperfect tense;
- the relative pronouns: *qui* and *que*.

These matters receive collective mention here from the point of view that they all responded satisfactorily and to some degree successfully to grammar-implicit teaching. In most cases this implied a response based on 'familiarity' resulting from frequent encounter and/or from being related to vocabulary rather than to any actual grammar. Nouns, adjectives and comparatives/ superlatives responded to repetitive and accentuated application. The learners simply became familiar with them, including their rule-exceptions. They used their powers of inference and analogy to clarify them further. The pronouns, however, received intensive teaching in the G-I mode (M1) with appropriate grammar summaries for the G-E class learning by M2. Unfortunately, the French pronouns-grammar is large and is exacerbated further by the rules pertaining to their word order in relation to the verb. Only the two Sets One were able to tolerate the teaching of pronouns, but they were unable to sustain their internalisation of it and carry it forward as a working concept for use as knowledge. They began with *moi* and *toi* which they used for all purposes along with one or two other pronouns like *il*; *elle*; *ils*, for example. *Nous* and *vous* caused some confusion and were often used interchangeably. In any case, the majority of the learners ended up with, and continued to apply, the pronouns they had started out with, as though the interval of teaching and learning had never occurred!

The method M was applied to the teaching of the imperfect tense and to *qui* and *que*. The imperfect was usually a straightforward formation to teach. It seemed ideally suited, indeed, to M or any other method, having a single procedure defining its structure and only one exception to its rule, namely *être*. However, though the lessons were well delivered and apparently meaningful, the only longer term application of this tense was made in terms of lexical items, as it were, such as *avait/avaient*; *était/étaient*; *allait/allaient*; *faisait/faisaient*. These seemed to satisfy the learners' needs (the first two items having implications also for the pluperfect tense later). The interaction of the perfect and the imperfect tenses defeated most of the learners, however, since their knowledge of this interaction in the L1 was undeveloped. Finally, *qui* and *que*, though carefully taught by M, defied the learners' powers of comprehension. They knew what they meant, but not when to use the one in preference to the other. This was because of their inability to recognise a subject from a direct object. Not even the grammar summary in English could clarify this difference for the G-E top set. Accordingly, these relative pronouns were decided by hunch, plainly with a 50% chance of success.

A note on the use of grammar summaries in G-E teaching (M2)

My main concern in this chapter has been to reveal, through selected examples of lessons described in a few broad brush strokes, the department's task of delivering the foreign language syntax and grammar by the grammar-implicit teaching approach construed by myself on our behalf as M. I have only briefly alluded to the L1 grammar summaries and consolidation procedures which were the added factor X feature in the cases of the G-E classes taught by M2. Teachers do not need to be reminded how this procedure was addressed! It may suffice to confirm at this point that these summaries were administered regularly in L1 terms admitting metalinguistic jargon. They involved oral discussion of the linguistic agendas that had been covered, followed up by fully explanatory written notes. The coursebook summaries which accompanied every unit of work were in any case at the learners' disposal and were often incorporated by the teacher in her script. They appeared as 'grey block' grammatical matter at intervals within the unit as well as in the form of end-of-unit 'summaries'. They were alluded to by the teacher and made an integral part of the L1 grammar consolidation process, in order to strengthen the role and the effect of the factor X device. **Considering also that individual grammatical agendas were repeatedly returned to our attention on the subject's spiral curriculum, it is clear that the L1 grammar summary mechanism was substantial enough to become a methodological discriminator.**

Lessons featuring learner-centred activities

TEACHING AND LEARNING THROUGH PLAY

In its simplest form play is turn-taking. This is a normal feature of the classroom, but we used it in the AR as a standard approach for ensuring that not only the 'good' learners but also the lazy, anxious, slow and diffident joined in and remained on task. We were concerned to ensure that **all** learners should claim their right to some time and involvement. Their levels of topic comprehension were highlighted while the teacher could judge simultaneously the apparent success or failure of her delivered agenda. Turn-taking was alternated often in my own classroom with the 'pick a victim' technique (*choisis un victime!*) of engaging all learners, with no 'victim' being picked twice before all class members had taken a turn. This took away the pressure from the teacher who so often appears to 'pick on' individuals in the class. It avoids the real risk of victimisation and reduces inhibitions. It is a far better idea that the teacher starts a class-round, picks the first (reliably able and confident) 'victim' to perform, say, an item in a time sequence, or to answer a question, and allows that 'victim' to choose a successor on delivering a correct response.

Games

As a general rule, young people love to play games. The play ethic infuses the foreign language lesson with a sense of expectation and a degree of enthusiasm, if the learners are allowed to anticipate that an area of time, however minor, is going to be incorporated on certain occasions for play purposes. The class members can be relied upon to invent new games or to apply themselves cheerfully to enacting old chestnuts like *Charades*; *What's My Line?*; *Give Us A Clue* (which film, book, play, TV programme?); *Hangman* (played on the blackboard, OHP, flipchart). Youngsters adore using the teacher's props and, in so doing, they place themselves out at the front, on task, with the potential to feel more self-confident and less threatened than may usually be the case. *Bingo* (*Lotto*), a favourite activity, is especially easily associated with prizes. It does not simply practise numbers, but almost any other grammar as well, whether it has already been encountered or is new and begging to be introduced (see p.48).

In my own classroom I discovered that Lotto was an excellent ploy for practising any grammar, like the integrated tensework above. In discussing the game-procedures, arrangements and prize choices, nouns, noun plurals, adjectives, demonstrative articles and pronouns, a broad range of interrogatives and also adverbs were given a practice-ground. Although it became a favourite game, especially since I made sure to equip myself with a professional-looking board, smart number-tabs and real Bingo tickets, I could not use this game all the time. Other *jeux de société* were used in a similar way in order to ring the changes. Some were bought in as games for extending the FL vocabulary, while others were made by the teachers or the learners or adapted from familiar and standard favourites like *Cluedo, Trivial Pursuit, What's My Line?, Happy Families*, etc.

T	*Alors, vous avez vos carnets de tickets? Oui? ... Très bien ... Qui n'a pas payé son entrée au jeu de deux pence?*
P1	*Alan. Alan n'a pas.*
T	*Alan n'a pas payé. Tu n'as pas de monnaie aujourd'hui Alan? ... Il faut prêter à Alain la monnaie. Oui? Qui peut faire ça? Qui peut lui prêter ... donner les deux pence?*
P2	*Moi, voilà.*
T	*Excellent. Alors, combien avons-nous maintenant dans la cagnotte?*
P3	*Soixante pence.*
T	*Et la dernière fois? Nous avons eu combien?*
P3	*Cinquante-six pence.*
T	*Qui a gagné cet argent, alors? Louise?*
Louise	*Greg. Il a gagné.*
T	*Et qui va gagner cette fois? Aujourd'hui? Samantha?*
Samantha	*Je ne sais pas.*
T	*Qui **veut** gagner? **voudrait** gagner? Toi, Neil?*
Neil	*Oui, je voudrais.*
T	*Tu auras soixante pence. Qu'est-ce que tu vas acheter plus tard?*
Neil	*Deux barres de chocolat. Euh ... oui, chocolat.*
T	*Excellent. Maintenant, jouons!*

Play is the best method of encouraging people to involve themselves, participate and learn through exploration and discovery. If handled correctly, there should be no perceived threat to any learners. Neither should any learner feel isolated, for there should always be a pair/group/team principle involved and an ethos of fun, therefore enjoyment. Extremely shy learners retain the right to step back but invariably make some gains, even so. The teacher, meanwhile, must lead by example, then lead from behind, as it were. The pupils will attempt to infer the language sequences which make the teacher's own attempt work well. Alternatively, they will try to recycle or reinvent them through analogy, in order to activate their individual or collective responses when taking their turns.

ACTIVITIES OF A HIGHER ORDER CREATIVITY

Not only do young people usually possess a creative talent and the imagination to activate it, they also feel – just as adults do – that there is a 'masterpiece' developing within them, waiting to be realised. This may be a play for actors, a song for singers, a story or a poem for readers, a film or a TV production for a viewing audience. And so on. I experienced examples of all of these work modes in my classroom during – and since – the AR. There were no lengths that budding artists would not go to in order to demonstrate their 'creative genius'. They generated a lot of pleasure and amusement, as well as demonstrating measurable amounts of good French language conveyed on steadily improving syntax and grammar. At the least, the more modest, less self confident and least talented made their contributions to the creative arena through individual or co-operative exposés, often delivered as tell-and-show demonstrations. Their end products emerged after much work on their part and subtle, low-key correction by the teacher, e.g.:

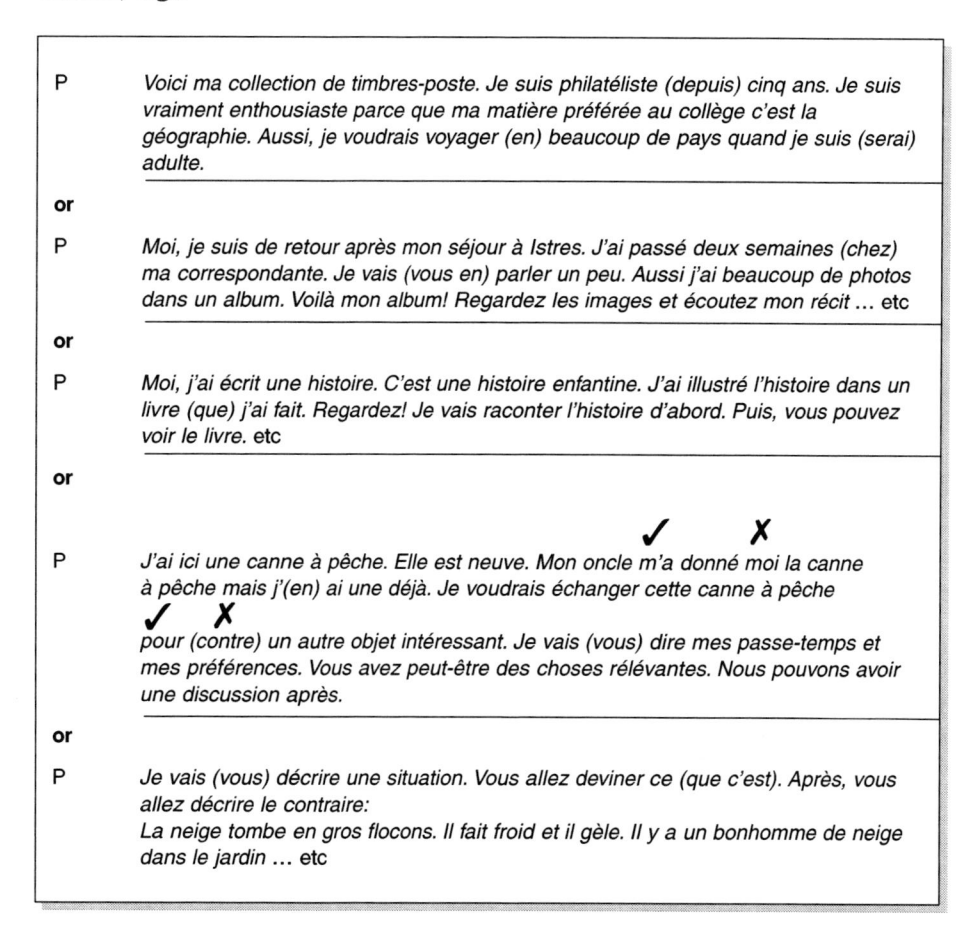

P	*Voici ma collection de timbres-poste. Je suis philatéliste (depuis) cinq ans. Je suis vraiment enthousiaste parce que ma matière préférée au collège c'est la géographie. Aussi, je voudrais voyager (en) beaucoup de pays quand je suis (serai) adulte.*
or	
P	*Moi, je suis de retour après mon séjour à Istres. J'ai passé deux semaines (chez) ma correspondante. Je vais (vous en) parler un peu. Aussi j'ai beaucoup de photos dans un album. Voilà mon album! Regardez les images et écoutez mon récit ... etc*
or	
P	*Moi, j'ai écrit une histoire. C'est une histoire enfantine. J'ai illustré l'histoire dans un livre (que) j'ai fait. Regardez! Je vais raconter l'histoire d'abord. Puis, vous pouvez voir le livre. etc*
or	
P	*J'ai ici une canne à pêche. Elle est neuve. Mon oncle m'a donné ✓ moi ✗ la canne à pêche mais j'(en) ai une déjà. Je voudrais échanger cette canne à pêche ✓ pour ✗ (contre) un autre objet intéressant. Je vais (vous) dire mes passe-temps et mes préférences. Vous avez peut-être des choses rélévantes. Nous pouvons avoir une discussion après.*
or	
P	*Je vais (vous) décrire une situation. Vous allez deviner ce (que c'est). Après, vous allez décrire le contraire:* *La neige tombe en gros flocons. Il fait froid et il gèle. Il y a un bonhomme de neige dans le jardin ... etc*

Clearly, an unlimited number of language scenarios can be invented in a similar manner to those featured above. They can be the work of more than one author, moreover. They are usually greatly enjoyed and prove very beneficial in special ways when they are generated out of shared effort. Some, though not all, of those offered above were features of my AR. Some are post-AR products. My own ability to incite active agendas of that kind has grown and improved as a result of my relevant efforts across my career, but particularly as a result of my concentrated efforts during the three years of applying the AR.

The following larger-scale creative agendas are, however, exclusively the product of the action research. I reserved them for use as part of our Year 11 work, knowing that by then the grammatical syllabus would have been completed (implying also the sundry revisitations) and that we could revise it through incorporating it in each of these major exercises:

(i) **A cake making exercise** (*Comment faire un gâteau*)

(ii) **Blind Date with Cilla Black** (*Rendez-vous-surprise avec votre hôtesse de cérémonie, Mam'selle Cilla Black!*)

(iii) **Poetry writing** for entry into the national poetry competition, run in 1994 for the first time by MGP in collaboration with the Bristol and West of England Comenius Centre and held at the CILT headquarters in London.

These features demanded considerable preparation and practice, to the extent that we had to set up several-after school workshops for the people involved in order to complete the exercises and eventually stage them in the classroom with the classes as the audience. The medium M was applied as the strict rule in the workshops, as in the classroom, for the conveying of the business.

- **The cake making exercise** This was done with each of my two Sets One, the one baking banana bread and the other a rich fruit cake. Sadly, it failed in my own critical estimation as a lesson plan for grammar revision, due to my cardinal misjudgment in placing myself as the agenda demonstrator in each case. This meant that I dominated the language as well as the activity, even eclipsing Kirsty of the G-I class and Peter of the G-E class, who had so gamely taken on the challenging star roles as the cooks. However, both classes enjoyed being video-filmed at work and later having an excellent party. This item remained a great favourite with the learners. In spite of my own reservations, they deemed it a long-lasting success on the grounds of its visual and practical impact. The exercises, generated out of the preparations and the video-recorded activity, are placed in Appendix A at the end of this book (p.121).

- *Rendez-vous surprise* was organised and performed by my own two top sets G-E and G-I. They each established committees to decide upon script writers and role players, but the generation of interesting ideas for the scripts depended upon the contributions made, in class, by the bulk of the class (overseen by the teacher, using M) in each case. Whereas the members of one class adhered to, and almost mimicked, the last 'Blind Date' programme they had seen, the other class made up its own school-based, very eccentric, zany and funny original text. An extract from one of the texts (and its exercises) is included as a creative work sample in Appendix A (p.125). This may help to clarify this item as the grammar teaching opportunity that it was perceived to be. Like the cake baking programme, my classes 'loved doing it'. It was a lot of fun but extremely challenging. They had to dig deep in their banks of learning and ingenuity in order to provide the levels of vocabulary and grammatical support that were vital to this agenda's successful completion.

- **Participating in the national poetry-writing competition** If there is anything that the children of my school do with enthusiasm, it is to compete artistically or in sports events. They acquit themselves very well in these senses and emerge invariably as worthy natives of a North East community which has realised its generous share of star performers. As part of my own MFL work with children, and long before the NC expressed interest in poetry writing as an exercise, I have always written poetry. I have developed a knack of getting poems out of learners very easily. I simply announce a poetry writing period and – often to my own amazement – the first drafts come in. Many poems are light-heartedly or perhaps humorously written. However, the occasion of writing a poem in a foreign language also potentially equips a young person with the opportunity to divulge a personal secret or express thoughts of a private, sometimes burdening nature. In writing it down the secret is out in a way, but kept confidential in the foreign language encasement. The poems invariably require a large investment of micro-work in order to bring them into a state of accuracy as language exercises and to do justice to the spirit of the poetry that they hold. This gives rise to valuable opportunities, in which individuals can claim their right to some personal time and attention and from which they can make real gains.

The poetry writing competition that Kate entered from her AR classroom in 1994 did not allow direct assistance from the teacher. Therefore I applied the 'grammar-implicit' principle in order to persuade her to embellish her early efforts until, in a systematic development, her poem assumed the beauty which ultimately impressed the competition judges. The finished version is attached as the third sample in Appendix A (p.129). It features a number of interesting characteristics concerning its young writer:

1. She wrote out of her own experiences. This made her want to do the exercise more than any other reason that one could imagine, namely – she was in love for the first time, or imagined being in love for the first time.

2. She liked poetry and sometimes tinkered about with it for its own sake.

3. She had collected one or two poetic images out of poems that she had already familiarised herself with. These became a ready made part of her investment in her own poem (aspects of this imagery will seem familiar to the reader, too).

4. She adored music, especially classical music, and already had a fixed tune in her head. She had recently developed an enthusiasm for this tune and it refused to go away.

   Clearly, it helped her to have a musical vehicle for her poem-in-the-making. The classical tune which so occupied her attention provided her with a mood/atmosphere, length of line and stanza, cadence, etc and it implied the need, as it turned out, for higher order lexis through which to do it justice.

5. At the time of deciding to create a competition poem, Kate was occupied in her French class with the conditional tense, its integrated use with the imperfect, the use of *si* and *quand* and the tenses which these require the

attendant verbs to take. This had been a difficult Year 11 agenda to deliver and appreciate by M. However, it had the quality and attraction that merited an important place in Kate's poem, as is immediately witnessed on reading it.

Striving, committed students are the most rewarding students of all. Kate was, indeed, such a student. Her poem, *'Premier amour'*, remains for me the 'jewel in the crown' of the grammar-implicit (M) plan. It demonstrates the distance that **can** be travelled by a junior FL learner from a heavily faulted but comprehensible, enthusiastic and malleable starting point to a near perfect and artistically satisfying finish. The method? One founded on persuasion, manipulation, encouragement, vision, self esteem, motivation, excellent pupil-teacher rapport and a weird system of treating and correcting a pupil's work related with the practice of M, in Kate's case M2, e.g.:

réfléchis-y!	erreur!	✗ ! ☹ !	☺ ! ✓ !
oui, enfin!	mieux!	pas mal!	excellent !
malchoisi!	bien choisi!	mal écrit!	
dictionnaire!	vocabulaire!	grammaire!	
participe passé!	pronom!		

The AR teaching methods (M1 and M2) in practice: summary and conclusion

In agreeing to make the base method for our NC experimental teaching M and to elaborate it to M + X in order to facilitate a contrastive study in teaching approaches, my colleagues and I understood that we must adhere to the methodological principles involved and so protect the integrity of the experiment. At the same time, we were obliged to deliver the French curriculum to its GCSE goal in an effective way.

- Teaching by M involved:
  - teaching wholly in the target language;
  - conveying grammatical agendas by implicit means, ideally without disclosing the grammar and explaining it as a separate (or disembodied) agenda.

- Using the factor X involved:
  - adding concise L1 grammar summary, spoken and written, to designated classes, to conclude and consolidate teaching which had featured a grammatical content.

- Defining 'grammar' involved:
  - identifying and addressing the **specified syllabus** of grammar that was the content of the GCSE examination course, as that to be taken over by the teachers for treatment in the action research. (Pronunciation, punctuation and spelling were the aspects of grammar which were given over entirely and unquestioned to M. They have received no mention in this account, accordingly.)

The smaller matters of pedagogical grammar were easily addressed through M, since they often modelled themselves as items of vocabulary and became familiar elements of the learners' language-use over time. However, the **verbs and tenses** agendas were extremely large and complex. This was especially true of the **perfect tense as a single item** and the interactive practice involving **two or more tenses or two past tenses as a collective item**. Some grammar-based teaching had necessitated a revised and extended notion of M, allowing a kind of explicit treatment by the teacher without involving the use of actually graphic and prescriptive L1 explanation or of metalinguistic terminology. The device of L1 grammatical summary with notes continued to be the extra treatment provided exclusively for the G-E classes, learning by M2. It was clear that without some form of amplification, such as highlighting, colour coding, clarification of time principles, and so forth, the verbs syllabus threatened to become systematically frustrated and, ultimately, irretrievably lost to the learners. The learners were in the position of having this convoluted and dense syllabus thrust upon them within the limited environment, the overpopulated classes and the inadequate time-scales which formed the background to their High School MFL curriculum. Thus they were offered the very antithesis of the conditions needed to support the immersion learning style that we were supposed to be mimicking in the L2 (namely the questionable time-schedule of 3 x 50 minutes per week, and the absence of adult and junior FL speakers in their surroundings, alluded to at an earlier juncture).

Somehow the present, perfect and future tenses had to be kept clear of confusion, since the correct comprehension and accurate production of meaning, crucial to the interactive/communicative purpose of the learners' course, are often influenced by these features of time. The imperfect is usually more easily expendable at this level, since its most frequently used instances can be absorbed in the manner of familiarised vocabulary. This is just as well, since the average learner has enough to do to cope with the perfect which dominates the past tense syllabus, arguably, and is, with the future, the grammar item which distinguishes the higher achievers from lower achievers in the GCSE. Quite simply, however, occupied at this level of their learning, and with no or little diagnostic understanding of the composition and function of their L1 to advise and sustain them in their L2 endeavours, youngsters may manage to recognise the three most distinct concepts of time (present, past as perfect and future) and perceive the need to apply them in order to negotiate a temporal context for a communication. However, the appearance of further tenses frustrates the convenient logic of the time grammar, demanding a more refined perception for the L2 purposes than the learner has acquired in terms of the L1. The methodologist, working to GCSE, must proceed carefully with the teaching brief and fulfil the teacher's responsibilities sympathetically, with the learners' needs and difficulties in mind.

A number of techniques, strategies, devices, mechanisms, tricks, ploys, materials and agendas used in effecting my AR methodological plan have been, as it were, paraded in this and earlier chapters. None of these things need be summarised again here. However, I believe one thing is clear: my personal understanding of the terms 'explicit' and 'implicit' in relation to foreign language grammar teaching and learning seems to me to differ from the way in which some others view these matters. For me 'explicit' FL grammar teaching means the implementation of a deductive, overt, didactic approach, conveyed to learners in the L1 terms. In this mode the FL grammar agenda is disembodied, analysed, explained and written up in L1 metalinguistic terms, and practised in exercises. The aim is then to re-embed it, i.e. the 'grammar' learnt, in the learners' increasing FL resource, ready for use. This final stage is known to be the crucial leap that young learners have difficulty in making. The method has a long history of use and has provoked a long history of debate, for it does not inevitably create able and confident language users. Hence the National Curriculum wishes teachers to try an alternative approach. My vision of this has been explored in my research and in part in this book.

The grammar-implicit teaching style, in its ideal form, is an **inductive** one which depends upon exposure to the language being learnt, upon practice and the notion of familiarity as the base on which one's language competence and performance develop. Perhaps then the case could be argued in support of applying a consolidating L1 grammar summary, made in the manner shown in my M2 which featured the factor X as a clarifying agent. Not all grammar points would require this, I feel sure.

The idea of using the 'tabula rasa' beginning and encouraging the natural acquisition of the L2, aided and abetted by the benefits of the 'immersion' and 'exposure' principles, is a laudable one. However, its immediate enemies are the serious constrictions of time, space, setting and cast of players. These constraints (together with class sizes) have featured in earlier discussions, but are repeated here, since they conspire persistently against naturalistic, i.e. genuinely 'implicit' foreign language acquisition. The result so often is that some short cuts to the learning must be found. The strategies that I have used and demonstrated in my compulsion to emphasise new grammar which featured in my teaching programme are, as I have already remarked, often viewed by other published writers as explicit, without, however, this necessarily meaning 'deductive' in their interpretation.

In spite of all the complications which set in to affect the AR, I and my colleagues made a clear and positive effort to differentiate between the two teaching styles that were crucial to our work. Our care in defining, employing and refining them was intense and continuous. We were, indeed, involved with real classroom practice in which we were seriously testing the wisdom of the NC proposal for a better future for MFL with greater success for learners. The testing ground was to be the GCSE results of our AR year group 'guinea pigs'. These results are yet to be considered. This will be done after I have examined the attitudes and responses to the AR teaching experience of its teacher and learner participants.

Chapter 5

The teachers' attitudes and perspectives during the action research

It was the conversion into active teaching of the G-I principle (described by ULEAC in a 1995/96 prospectus as the 'new generation's methodology') which stirred reactions among the teachers and learners who participated in my action research. Their collective disposition was monitored through discussions, recordings and questionnaires at regular intervals during the three-year course of the experiment. I have been able to draw on this evidence in order to inform my reflections on G-I and G-E since that time, in general terms, or when my remit has been to examine the viewpoints of the teachers and the learners. This I now do in this current chapter and in the next.

The responses of the action research teachers to their grammar-implicit teaching brief

For the purpose of convenience and economy, the teachers' responses are discussed in this chapter in stages. The sequence of the AR's content development will be adhered to for this purpose, since this was very often the underlying structure and provocation of the reactions which have merited discussion.

ANTICIPATING THE ACTION RESEARCH

In May 1991 I started negotiations with my colleagues on matters relating to the AR, the reasons for it and their roles within it. During talks, I gave them files containing reference and explanation sheets on the NC policy for MFL, with its implications for methodological procedures: the position and importance of comprehensive TL application and the new thinking on 'grammar' teaching. I explained the usefulness to us and our MFL department of using the three-year interval 1991 to 1994 for pre-NC dry-run purposes. I noted my colleagues' reactions as follows:

The teachers' attitudes and perspectives during the action research — 57

- At first there was shock without surprise. We had mooted the experiment for a time, but we were now making it actual.

- This was followed by some expression of anxiety. The work would necessitate recording lessons and make us audibly if not visually accountable to each other – and to ourselves. If the ideal was to be preserved, there would be no escape from the agreed plan. We would be seen to fail or pass the tests imposed on our teaching abilities but also on each individual's sense of commitment and integrity. Our personal inadequacies would become clear to others. Our strengths might not compensate. I, as Head of Department, was better placed than the others to take the inevitable stress and discomfort and to stand accountable for the practice stall I set out. The AR was my particular creation. It was extremely important to me at both a personal and professional level, and I was prepared to dig as deep as was necessary, in order to give it its planned life-span. However, the others were not its author and their commitment and loyalty to it were going to be seriously tested. My colleagues felt these fears in anticipation of the AR, when it was only a principle. They expressed more concern, therefore, in imagining it converted into a long-term practice, despite their having used the teaching methods required of them already in the past, albeit in a fairly desultory way and to a far smaller degree than was needed now.

- Eventually, compliance was established and a positive rationale for the AR was agreed. The exercise of trialling the NC methods was one based on common sense and implied real advantages for the present and future work of the department and for the individuals teaching in it.

- A change of mood ensued. Anxiety, uncertainty, self doubt, diffidence and the fear of inadequacy made space for a sense of expectation, the hope for an increased self confidence to come. The notion of exploring, ahead of the NC inception, the particular enigma of the G-I method and of testing the NC's assumption of the value of this to MFL teaching and learning seemed a relevant and sensible one, issuing a well timed opportunity.

The teachers' feedback on their experience in the classroom

THE TEACHERS' RESPONSES BY THE END OF OCTOBER 1991

These were collated at the time of discussion following the completion of Unit One (*Tricolore 3*). This had focused on the perfect tense, *devoir* and the 'negatives'. Our discussion aired the following shared thoughts and reactions:

- It was proving difficult to adhere to one teaching style without wanting to take rule breaking **diversions** to target.

- Whatever one's plans and arrangements were for the **process**, one was always inevitably seriously concerned about the **product**.

- Teaching one's agenda, practically, by inductive means, using exercises, games and other strategies, was an extremely difficult ambition to stage and maintain in practice.

- The whole G-I arrangement, i.e. M as M1 and as the base and main structure of M2, was difficult to articulate, support and sustain.

- The grammatical agenda attached to the first unit of work was a ponderous one. The learners had demonstrated:
  - an inability to grasp the underlining concepts;
  - a lack of awareness of the matching L1 concepts;
  - a lack of learning skills (which disturbed us!);
  - a lack of awareness of their responsibility for their own learning as partners with their teachers in the teaching/learning process.

- Specifically, the perfect tense agenda, with its layers of sub-agenda, had been a frustrating experience at the Unit One visitation. There had been no widespread evidence on the learners' part of cross-referencing with the L1. The general lack of their ability to (covertly) do this had frustrated pupils and teachers alike.

- The grammar of Unit One had been covered in the Middle Schools in the year(s) prior to transfer. However, the learners of the year group as a whole had been unable to carry forward any (measurable) knowledge or experience of it. Very few indeed admitted to having any recall even through recognition. This told us something about the process of recall in the adolescent learner for potential consideration at a later date.

- We discussed the nature of the year group as a perceived (relatively speaking) low attaining and unmotivated one. We also consulted the relevant QSL findings (Quality of Student Learning, researched by the University of Newcastle at the time) and the opinions of the pastoral staff on the prognosis for the development of this AR year group. As our experience of the year group increased, we felt there were benefits in referring to other sources as a means to confirm, and at least to compare, the impressions that we were forming.

THE TEACHERS' RESPONSES BY CHRISTMAS 1991

Our discussions were held following the teaching of the future tense contained in the second teaching unit's agenda:

- My colleagues reported having encountered the same difficulties as myself in delivering this grammar agenda. We decided that there were four principal reasons for our shared disappointment. These concerned our efforts (a) with the teaching by M of the future tense, specifically, and (b) with the teaching by M in general. The four points were as follows:

1. The clear structure which makes the future tense ideal for didactic teaching, had seemed to equip it also for an unproblematic passage with M. This did not happen, perhaps because we were too confident and possibly too complacent in our appreciation of this grammatical item.

2. It was probable that our own backgrounds as explicit (deductive) and at best eclectic practitioners got in the way of our efforts with M. Our 'conscious' adapting teacher-persona wanted to deliver by M, whereas our unconscious or subconscious habitual classroom persona instinctively and automatically wanted to effect our accustomed styles. The two had to collide.

3. The theory and the practice of M was becoming an ever increasing problem. As one person put it: 'I can work a thing out in my head and in my intention, but it slips through my grasp in practice.' Then she explained the worst aspect of the theory/practice divide: 'It is especially frustrating, just plain awful actually, when I perceive that the class is not with me anyway. The agenda and my resolve just hit the floor and I wonder where I can get my back-up from – what I can fall back on – if I can't break with M at times when my attempt with M has let me down.'

4. Having dabbled with M on occasions in the past, we thought we could equate our slight experience of it with the input by M required of us in the AR. However, we were learning as we proceeded that we could not decant enough potent experience from our former experimentations with M to give authority to our serious efforts with it, and our intended sustained practice of it, in the AR.

- The catalogue of difficulties and impediments affecting good practice using M, which we seemed able to report on at this stage, informed us of a long-overlooked and by-passed reality of teaching and of our approach to it. First of all, we get to a point, as teachers, at which we risk failing to stop, reflect, analyse and, as it were, 're-group'. When this is the case, we become, perhaps, complacent and cease to take into account the issues surrounding the teaching methods, approaches and styles which we apply in our practice. Thus these become our personal signature in the course of time. At least the AR and the need to use M was well placed and well primed to redress the balance in this respect, because we could not apply M without a lot of reflection, conscious planning and resourceful preparation.

- An important awareness emerged, curiously, with all of us AR teachers at this time. We decided that there seemed to be 'right times' in the development of learners for certain items of their syllabus to be acceptable to their learning mechanisms and conceptual development. There were also, therefore, by analogy, 'wrong' times for certain matters to be learnt and 'right' and 'wrong' times for the teaching to be done, accordingly. We discussed these as 'the learners' points of preparedness' or 'the learners' readiness' to accept and internalise concepts. We realised that if we taught a matter that the learners were not conceptually ready for and their minds were not naturally and genuinely receptive to, then we could teach until the proverbial cows came home and by whatever method we wished to employ, and our effort would be to little or to no avail. This was, we realised, potentially hugely wasteful in classrooms in which the agenda is not moved on. However, we conceded also that more highly skilled use of M in which the **grammar content is not graded** (and the NC advocates this very principle!) could, and logically should, address these problems with positive results and to everyone's advantage in the MFL classroom.

- Our speculations about the teaching method M extended the previous point and produced an optimistic outlook for the future: If, through experience which improves practice, we were to eventually establish M as the method for use in our MFL classrooms, we could perhaps neutralise the vexations that occur for the learners at times when they are not disposed to understand their syllabus. The vexations which are implied for the teachers may be dissolved also with the disappearance of the persistent but incorrect equation: **teaching** equals **learning**. This equation is so often expressed in any teacher's perplexed protest: 'If I've taught it, why don't they know it?'

M, our interpretation of the advocated NC teaching method, could be the instrument to bring equanimity to MFL teaching and learning in the course of time. After all, it was articulated through full target language use which itself had a **whole grammar** base and content.

The teachers' responses by the Spring Term of 1992

The third phase of the Year 9 work was designed as a tense-consolidation programme and contained no 'new' agenda. It was anticipated, therefore, that the teachers would be able to use this interval as the opportunity for experimenting freely with M and for shedding some of the tensions that had built up around it. My own state of satisfaction, commitment and motivation was positive and improving all the time in my work with the Sets One and Four. Therefore, I was disappointed to learn of the persistent and by now quite intense concerns that my colleagues were struggling with in the contexts of their middle status settings. They clarified these concerns on this occasion as follows:

- Their pupils were unable to formally or informally identify a 'verb' from any other grammatical component, say a 'noun' or an 'adjective'. It followed, therefore, that they were unable to distinguish among the tenses of the verbs and as always had no success in mentally seeking to evoke parallels in English. Indeed, it appeared they had, in the main, rarely experienced an English grammar syllabus raised to their awareness in their English subject classrooms. Their English was extended in the classroom but was mainly the sum of the L1 that they had accrued outside, each on a personal level, as young individuals over their time since birth, living unequal lives in unequal circumstances. In current times, the classroom activities, which characterised their pursuit of English as a school subject, relied upon this accoutrement as the medium to articulate and satisfy them.

- The learning of the foreign language (French) was made plain as an irksome task, which many learners resisted and would rather not have to do. My colleagues conceded that, whereas the programme of the teaching and learning was not disproportionate with the GCSE requirements, the **assessment plan** which we had established in relation to the AR was, indeed, too onerous. In agreeing to screen it, adjust it and cut it back for future stages of the course, I hoped to relieve us, and our classes in particular, of some of our overload. This might allow us as a team to perhaps 'lighten up' with respect to M also.

- As a teaching team we discussed the importance of a method to ensure classroom success and a good end-product. Given my colleagues' fundamental reservations about M in practical terms, explored earlier, it might have been anticipated that M would be ultimately responsible for the low performance, the reluctance to work and the failure to comprehend the foreign language on the part of too many learners in their classes. However, I was personally faring better with M than were my colleagues. I was happier with my remit with M and I was happier with the attitudes of my classes. In both instances this may have had much to do with the fact that my top sets were somewhat better disposed to the idea of learning a foreign language than were the middle sets which resented the 'MFL for all' ruling in principle. As for the two Sets Four, they were typically flattered that they were allowed to do some French and set about it with a show of enthusiasm. Our observations at this time caused us to speculate that a specific method (unless it is extreme by nature, as 'grammar-translation' had proved to be) may, after all, have less than is imagined to do with learners' success in the subject. Certainly, pupils' positive attitudes and their state of motivation – or the absence of these – seem to be a major influence. In positive form they were vital factors affecting the quality of their performances and their prospects of attaining satisfactory examination grades.

- This much was clear (above rationale), but less clear was still the relationship of a particular **teaching method to learners' motivation** and to their effecting good **learning strategies** and producing successful **outcomes**. From my position and work with my own parallel classes, I was able to reflect further on this matter. I was particularly fascinated by the differences discernible between the two Sets One, as the sets which would work in the AR for its full duration. The G-I Set One was apparently attitudinally homogeneous compared with its G-E counterpart, at this stage of its 'career' in GCSE French, at least. Its internal group relationships were excellent. In the G-E situation a number of weaker, potentially negative attitudes were noticeable. This point has interesting implications for what was proved much later about the two groups' **subject performances**: that the homogeneity was detectable in general academic terms with the group G-E and not with G-I! This development may have something reinforcing to offer in support of the point that is being made here! Personally, I was open-minded in my views on classroom success. For me this requires a method to combine with the generation of a satisfying subject experience and satisfactory outcomes for learners, developing out of positive classroom relationships. These relationships bring the best out of each group member and out of the teacher. They build high levels of **expectation, motivation, self-confidence, self-esteem** and the **will** (**ambition**) to do well. When these are in place, the method, as long as it is relevant to the course, is charged with the positive opportunity to be effective. Thus it may also appear that the method, being a self-proving 'good' method, is having a beneficial effect on results and has had, in the meantime, an enhancing influence on attitudes and relationships. Having encountered and reflected in this way on the puzzle of the 'chicken and the egg', and focusing again on the difficulties of teaching the middle sets, my colleagues and I decided at this stage to give credence to the following inference which our observations had led us to make:

Effective teaching	is reflected in
Satisfactory learning	which is due to
positive, whole class	**Relationships**
in which class members share....................	**Motivation**

The teachers' responses by Easter of 1992

These were conducted through the medium of a questionnaire on this occasion. I aimed to ascertain developments where my colleagues' work and outlooks were concerned, since our last discussion. Accordingly, I enquired as to:

- their satisfactions and/or concerns with the new work since then and with the assessment associated with it;

- whether they continued to understand the nature of the method M in its forms M1 and M2;

- whether they continued to use their M-based method;

- what problems, if any, they had encountered since the last discussion;

- what further observations they could make about their pupils' learning;

- what they could say about their pupils' performance and progress;

The teachers' attitudes and perspectives during the action research — 63

- which items of the grammatical teaching agenda they had taught best and worst by their selected method, and why they perceived this to be the case.

My colleagues' observations were collected and summarised as shown in the outline below:

REFERENCING THE QUESTIONS	THE TEACHERS' RESPONSES
1. The satisfactions	• **Assessment** had been cut back and was now manageable and in better ratio to the teaching. • **Learners' attitudes** were more positive, due to reduction of their test-weariness. • **Improved performance** in 'Listening' and 'Reading' was a welcome development.
2. The concerns	• **Continuing disappointment** in 'Speaking' and 'Writing'. • **Presentation of work** showed lack of pride, lack of care, etc. • French was branded too hard to really keep believing in it.
3. The methods	• Colleagues 1a and 1b understood the methods. • They were trying to apply the methods as before but each was becoming more and more explicit (1a in the L2 and 1b in the L1).
4. The application of the methods	• The difficulties were compounding. • Some grammar matters were more difficult than others to convey by M. • They had different perceptions from each other and from myself also as to what was (a) viable by M and (b) resistant to M, e.g. of the two G-I teachers, colleague 1a and myself, colleague 1a branded adjectives and plurals resistant to M, whereas I found them easily viable. In the case of colleague 1b, the issues of viability and resistance were beginning to threaten her sense of self-confidence and her confidence in M, to the extent that she over-employed the factor X and punctuated her lessons with frequent explicit discussion of the grammar content in English.

Referencing the questions	The teachers' responses (continued)
5. Problems emerging since the last discussion	All the difficulties prevailed still, as matters of: – **performance** – **relationships** – **motivation**, etc
6. The continuing discussion	• The learners' general lack of enthusiasm. • Their inability axnd/or reluctance to take responsibility for their own learning. • The management of M suffered as a result of the above two deficits. • Teachers now asked the question: **why is it wrong to explain grammar?** • Some more perceptive learners were simply asking: **why?** in relation to their work in class. • **Discernible progress** after this long in teaching by M1 or M2 had assumed a contradictory pattern: ✓ = more progress　✗ = less progress My own classes　G-I　and　　G-E Sets One　　　　　✓　　　　　✗ Colleagues 1a, 1b Sets Two　　　　　✗　　　　　✓

The teachers' responses by Whitsun 1992

Since it was thought that very little had changed, and that any commentary that could be made on the implementation and effects of M had been made already, little fresh discussion emerged at this stage. Unit Five of the coursebook was the final unit of the course stage, presently in place in the classrooms in its capacity also as the end-of-year's work. The grammatical agenda was the imperfect tense which, having an easily definable structure and only one exception to its general rule, was, in theory, easy to teach by M. However, the rationale for its application, the logic surrounding the questions **Why use it?** and **When to use it?** provoked considerable frustration for learners, therefore for the teachers also. My colleagues were far more concerned about this item than I was. I happily forged ahead, confident that my top set learners were more likely to find a use for it, arguably, than their middle-range learners. Colleagues 1a and 1b pressed for still further adjustments to the AR, in the light of these concerns.

THE TEACHERS' RESPONSES BY THE SUMMER OF 1992 (END OF YEAR 9)

The principal points of reflection were as follows:

- As a result of all the discussions throughout the year, and after consolidating the results of the regularly applied assessments and end-of-year examination, M seemed to emerge as a very viable proposition for use with upper set pupils, whereas it was thought to lead to a degree of misery with the middle status sets. For these classes it was, at the outset, irksome to have the target language grafted into lessons as the sole medium of the interaction.

- It was agreed that teaching by M asked a great deal of the teachers' expertise and could easily exclude the learners from a meaningful share of the classroom action. This would prevent them from assuming a real role in the interactive dialogue needed to characterise a purposeful teaching/learning partnership, which is judged to be desirable in the modern classrooms and is at the heart of the current methodological ideal.

- Everyone agreed that the successful use of M relied upon the teachers' incorporating the process of somehow (and effectively enough) raising matter to the learners' consciousness. It was indeed the need to do this and the procedures for doing it, which conspired against the teachers' ability to feel 'comfortable' with M.

- Thankfully, I emerged from the first year of the experiment with my enthusiasm undiminished and my grasp of M arguably still intact. Within this first year my G-I Set One had seemed to learn the subject **intuitively**, certainly in an unpremeditated way, whereas my G-E Set One had worked with a more **conscious, cautious** attitude. This could become a fuller statement, indeed, to witness my observation that the G-I Set One was **intuitively better at French** whereas, at this stage, the G-E Set One was **consciously better at grammar**! I was immediately interested to discover, over the course of time, whether this difference would prevail to characterise each set and distinguish them, the one from the other, or whether there would be further curves of change. More will be noted on this vital development in the results chapter. It holds the key, after all, to an understanding of the power of pure M or, conversely, of the need for an explicit component (such as the factor X) to raise M to its point of efficiency as the NC's advocated method for the delivery of a foreign language at GCSE level.

The above observations are a representative cross-section of those recorded as the first year's work with M went its course. The arrival of Year 10 as the second phase of the GCSE course, managed through the application of M, was anticipated as matter for discussion of a disclosing and clarifying nature in the same way.

66 — REFLECTIONS ON GRAMMAR-IMPLICIT LANGUAGE TEACHING

The teachers' responses by October 1992

- The middle-range pupils had returned to school somewhat disaffected after the summer break. Having faced an early Year 10 agenda of **adjectives** and **interrogative pronouns**, their teachers expressed acute disappointment, to say the least, over their general disinterest and a number of specific aspects of attitude such as the following:
  - lack of concentration in class;
  - lack of value/respect for the subject;
  - lack of willingness to learn;
  - resistance to their subject responsibilities;
  - general complacency;
  - failure to retain knowledge and to recall;
  - lack of awareness of patterns;
  - inability to perceive patterns;
  - inability to discriminate between what was correct and what was incorrect;
  - lack of 'hunch knowledge';
  - inability to apply the 'laws' of analogy;
  - inability to manage more than one item at a time, e.g. an adjectival agreement and a tense requirement.

- Although we were aware that this disaffection often sets in after Year 9, this was clearly enough to make even the most stout hearted weep! It was feared by colleagues 1a and 1b that the use of M might be responsible for the scale of the problem they described. Colleague 1a, teaching by M1, put her argument: 'Well, just how **do** you teach them? ... It's all very well to **imply** this is masculine, this is feminine, this is plural, etc as long as you are dealing with "regulars". But as soon as you get into the "irregulars" ... I found it impossible to teach them. I couldn't do it by the method (M as M1).'

- Both colleagues expressed themselves to be equipped by this point with enough experience of trialling M to take issue with our use of the principle of M as a viable and justifiable means of teaching a foreign language. They doubted whether **any** practitioner, however gifted or committed, could do justice to the brief of delivering the FL in its own medium with the grammar undeclared.

- The colleagues saw the essence of M to be its mercurial, potentially unstable nature. They found that this made it vulnerable to the variables and imponderables which beset it in their classrooms.

- They were discouraged further by the problems of resourcing M; of planning lessons plentifully, pliably and imaginatively in order to satisfy M; of using the foreign language flexibly at a number of ranges, and cunningly enough to guarantee the communication intended as a two-way process, appropriately interactive, therefore.

- The colleague 1b, who taught by M2 and was, therefore, expected to use the explicit grammar summary in English, was over-using the summary device and had to be asked to re-think her approach to it. She admitted that the theoretical rationale for the use of the factor X seemed perfectly viable, but she had found herself experiencing insurmountable difficulty with the whole of M2 and had extended the parameters of the grammar summary in order to help herself to deliver the lessons and her pupils to understand them. She freely admitted: 'I have attempted to do implicit teaching all along – and I just **could not do it!**'

- Both colleagues 1a and 1b shared the following impressions at this stage of our observations:

  - that, despite all accumulating experience, M remains very difficult to execute;

  - that the teacher is too often prone to making a potentially solo performance in M, leaving the class behind as an unequal or ironically silent partner in the work;

  - that the teacher, always in theory concerned that the learners should take responsibility for their own learning, through using M actually runs the risk of disabling or disempowering the learners, rather than enabling them to engage in the work and to interact in the general communicative 'exercise';

  - that M requires the teacher to be as much a facilitator as a didactic instructor, and some teachers with strongly didactic approaches find it difficult to adapt to this quite different style;

  - that, in the spirit of M, the lesson matter must be managed in a circumspect fashion so that it shapes up in the most natural way, allowing no seams and edges to show through. This tests and stretches the teacher's skill to the ultimate degree;

  - that the method M, as we had framed it, must be viewed realistically as (a) an unattainable ideal for some teachers, (b) a method for the gifted, versatile and self-confident perhaps and, therefore, (c) not a wholly feasible possibility for necessarily all teachers of current times. The circumstances and conditions in which teachers now work – the amount of bureaucracy alone; the often daunting sizes of the classes; the need to adapt their policies and approaches to the requirements of their individual schools, and to address themselves through their work to the repeatedly changing times; all such factors and more – conspire against their being able to commit all of the appropriate time and effort to the preparation, delivery and monitoring of the practical classroom agenda.

- The colleagues finally asked to be released from the AR exercise. This development came as no surprise to me, since I had observed the down-scale of their argumentation in our discussions since the start and had noted no really positive response to M other than their genuinely conscientious efforts and their willingness to 'give it a go' for the sake of the AR and in order to practise the tenets of the NC. They excused their decision via their concern for their classes:

- the classes seemed to have cut off from the work;
- it was impossible to encourage and motivate the pupils, when the teachers themselves felt discouraged and demotivated;
- it was a problem keeping the learners on task and on GCSE target.

• Of my two colleagues, colleague 1b was the more diffident of the two where the trialling of M in the AR was concerned. Her case for leaving the AR is inherent in the arguments just given. Colleague 1a, whose teaching method was M1, regretted having to give up her effort and her part in the AR, for in so doing she was relinquishing her opportunity to anticipate the reality of the NC, as mentioned. It also went against her grain to capitulate her part in any context. As a qualified and long experienced teacher, she felt she owed it to herself to stay with the AR. However, she felt even more strongly that she owed to her pupils more than she owed to herself. She and colleague 1b continued to make an input to the AR until the half-way stage which coincided with the February half-term of 1993. They then withdrew and continued the GCSE course with their classes, teaching by their own methods.

Conclusion to the teachers' discussions

The AR had given my colleagues a valuable experience in teaching methods by requiring them to explore one specific method, plan it out and implement it in their classrooms. This analytical and taxing exercise had uplifted them from their accustomed furrow and given them the opportunity to refresh their practice through reflection and alternative practical subject management. Each teacher discovered new things about the nature of the job she was accustomed to doing and about how she would be expected to do it in the future. My colleagues may have reached only the half-way point of the AR with M, but their gained insights were to relate with their long-term teaching goals, far beyond the completion of the AR. The questions which repeatedly dogged their practice – and, indeed, they haunt every teacher's practice – would no longer go unheeded, for my colleagues now knew that they were worth addressing and that they had come closer to providing responses to them, thanks to their participation in the AR. We all recognise such questions as part of each teacher's enquiry. Despite my having already alluded to them briefly, I repeat them here:

'If I have taught it, why haven't they learnt it?'

or 'If I have taught it, why don't they know it?'

or 'If I feel that my lessons were good (or poor), why do they often give the opposite verdict on them?'

At a much later date, after my colleagues had had time to settle down to their own way of doing things with their respective GCSE classes, I asked them to respond to a set of questions to update my perspective on their pupils' attitudes and learning.

My aim was to find out how much difference my colleagues' decision to leave the AR in favour of following their 'free' methods had made to their pupils' attitudes and performance. Their collective answer was simple and in its way satisfying. It is encapsulated below:

THE QUESTIONS	THE RESPONSES
1. Had the change of method from M positively affected the learners' attitudes to the subject?	**negative**
Did their current performance seem to have gained from the change in circumstances?	**negative**
Had the prospects for positive results in the GCSE improved?	**negative**
2. What benefits had they expected to encounter on leaving the restrictive AR?	**revitalisation of the classroom practice and of pupils' attitudes and prospects**
3. What proportion of these benefits had, in fact, come to fruition?	**no change**

On reflection and with the wisdom of hindsight, the colleagues 1a and 1b ultimately exonerated the method M (G-I) from the blame that they had assumed it to have in relation to their problems with their GCSE sets in French. Indeed, they were now clear that 'no teaching method is wholly accountable for learners' success or failure in a course of learning'. There was one further occasion in which we talked together on the subject of grammar-implicit teaching. The views that they expressed at this time were the result of the consolidation that time, experience and reflection bring. The content of this conversation is alluded to later (Chapter 8).

Finally, this chapter has concentrated in the main on the views and reactions of those who worked with me on the trialling of M in the AR. My own views and reactions were not always reflected in them, but rather they are dispersed throughout the whole of this book.

In any case, my own work in the AR benefited from my double privilege as the deeply motivated author of and potential profit-maker from the AR, and the teacher of two relatively higher status, more easily manageable, French groups. My relationship with the method under experimentation was much different to that of my colleagues, therefore.

Chapter 6

The responses of the action research learners

At half-termly or termly intervals during the three-year period of my action research, I extracted information from the responses to questions which I had put to the pu left me with the two Sets One, amounting to some 60 learners. In order to explore our pupils' attitudes to their FL learning brief and to discover their thoughts on the teaching methods which were applied by teachers in the classroom, I put regular questionnaires in place as the main research device. I then reinforced the inquiry through occasional group discussions and case-study interviews, all of which were audio-recorded. Clearly, my intention was to observe their perspectives on the methods that we applied, fashioned around the full use of the target language and the implicit, i.e. covert, delivery of its grammar; then, in its rightful context, the issue of the factor X. The pupils' responses were assembled and analysed for feedback purposes in the calendar sequence in which they were sought, before being assessed as a collective reaction in concluding the investigation. In the narrow scope of this chapter, I can chart some of the broader insights that this study of learners' attitudes brought us.

A selection of questionnaires and the learners' responses

THE FIRST QUESTIONNAIRE

This occurred during October/November 1991 on completing the work and assessment on *Tricolore 3* Unit 1 (the whole Year 9 intake is involved) and inquired into the following areas:

1. the pupils' state of self confidence in using the FL;
2. the perceived clarity of the lessons (performed in M);
3. their ability to name some items they had learnt;
4. the possible requirement for more teaching on specific items;
5. pupils' familiarity with the contents and layout of their textbooks;
6. whether the October tests had been perceived as easy or hard;

7. the number of pupils for whom the term 'grammar' was a concept which they could explain.

The responses to the first questionnaire

- The Sets One (G-I and G-E) were equally divided on claiming to have self-confidence or the lack of it in their management of the subject. However, the responses of the Sets Two showed only sparse self-confidence in this respect. This is significant, bearing in mind the systematic erosion in their participation in the experiment and their early capitulation.

- All the sets found their lessons clear, in general. Out of 161 pupils (including the Germanists), 24 answered in the negative on this; 78 attempted to name an item of the agenda that had been taught, most popularly the **perfect tense** and the **plurals of nouns** (the latter being a residue from the Middle School syllabus rather than a feature of the current work programme). There was some demand for more explanation, presumably grammar, and more skills practice, on a scale of 1:2 respectively.

- There was an overwhelmingly positive response to confirm familiarity with the coursebooks. Only 21 pupils out of 161 negated this.

- The learners of French (102) found their tests difficult, with 21 exceptions.

- Only two learners out of the 161 thought that they understood the term 'grammar' enough to define it.

THE SECOND QUESTIONNAIRE

This occurred during Christmas 1991, on completing the work and assessment on *Tricolore 3* Unit 2 (the whole Year 9 intake is involved) and explored the following areas:

1. pupils' perceived difficulties;
2. their recall of the last term's agenda;
3. their requirements, if any, of further teaching of particular items;
4. their assessment of the lessons viz pace, clarity;
5. pupils' understanding of the matters taught and their state of self confidence.

The responses to the second questionnaire

- The greatest difficulties were named as **structures**, **verbs** and some **themes** (e.g. travel).

- The most popular recall of the agenda of the previous term focused again on **structures**, **verbs** and some **themes**.

- **Structures**, **verbs** and some **themes** were deemed in need of extra teaching, moreover.

- The majority of the learners complained about the fast pace of the lessons and the overcrowded agenda.

- The overwhelming majority, i.e. 160/180 claimed to have clear memory of the previous term's agenda, but only 68/160 could attempt to describe it or name any of its features.

- 130/180 pupils claimed to be happy and self-confident in their MFL studies this time. (This implied a measure of contradiction in terms of the middle set pupils' responses.)

THE THIRD QUESTIONNAIRE

This occurred during February 1992, after completing the work and assessment on *Tricolore 3* Unit 3 (the whole Year 9 intake is involved) and concentrated on exploring the following matters:

1. what the pupils felt they knew most about in their FL studies;
2. what the pupils felt they knew least about;
3. whether the process of learning and using the FL was perceived to be the same for them as the process of 'learning' English;
4. whether the process of learning the FL had extended their understanding of English.

NB Questions 3 and 4 provoked particularly spirited returns from a large number of respondents. This is reflected in my analysis of responses.

The responses to the third questionnaire

- All the groups claimed to know most about the **present tense**. This was a residue of their Middle School syllabus, as also was their use of the term: **present tense**. Moreover (and ironically), there was very little competent use of the present tense in the Year 9 work.

- The majority of the group claimed to know least about the **perfect tense**; the G-I groups were, understandably, more numerical in this context than the G-E groups.

- To the question exploring the learning of L1 as compared to the learning of L2, the responses showed the following perceptions:

    – the G-I groups   7% found the processes the same
                            93% found the processes different;

- the G-E groups   27% found the processes the same
                     73% found the processes different;

- overall   17% found the processes the same
                     83% found the processes different.

The reasoning attached to this analysis featured similar arguments for both sides of the debate, however:

ENGLISH (L1)	FRENCH (OR L2)
• is easier • absorbs all of one's available time • surrounds the individual • is used flexibly • has been 'got' naturally • is 'traded' unconsciously • features in all contexts • it needs not be teacher-directed • there is no concern about L1 growth • it is a part of you, like a skin or a necessary body part; it is a habit • is used/understood at speed • (the processes of English are hidden (we are unaware of processes in L1 (L1 has no rules therefore no processes (there is nothing to process in L1 • English is an ocean of language • English is used at less speed • sounds are clear in English • we learn English at first hand an authentic context, setting • natural learning through use • it resources our lives • one is usually positive and uncritical about one's L1 • in English you can produce 'talk' for almost any context • in English you can edit your 'talk' as you go along • in English you can find ways around difficulties in 'talk'	• is very hard • is given very little time • is experienced in small packs • is used only in a number of set phrases • has been 'got' unnaturally • is premeditated before written or said • features in certain school contexts • it needs to be teacher-directed • there is always concern about L2 growth • it is not a part of you; you have to manufacture it and a need for it • use/comprehension are much slower • L2 is full of difficulties/problems) rules are implied even if not seen) • L2 is unnatural, contrived, forced • L2 is a drop in the ocean of language • French is made hard by its speed • sounds are indistinguishable in French • we learn French at second hand • an artificial (pretend) context, setting • pressure-learning through drills, exercises • it resources our lessons and subject tests • one is usually negative and critical about one's L2 • in L2 you can produce limited 'talk' for very few contexts • in L2 you are not flexible enough to edit your 'talk' • in L2 you can either 'say' it or you can't

- To the question about the effect of L2 learning upon L1 awareness the following response emerged:

The 'factions'	G-I	G-E
Yes, L2 learning affects L1 awareness	33%	28%
No, L2 learning does not affect L1 awareness	67%	72%

The principal arguments which this poll presented were as follows:

YES L2 LEARNING INFLUENCES L1	NO L2 LEARNING DOES NOT INFLUENCE L1
• You learn L2 consciously, therefore you think more about L1. • You discover items with special names and functions in L2 and you look for them in L1 as well. • L2 conditioning makes you proceed more fussily with L1. • L2 learning makes you realise that language is structured and L1 is therefore structured also. This comes as a surprise and changes your attitude to it. • You discover things about English that you did not know before, mainly that it is a complex system and not just made up of strings of words. • You learn a lot about L1 from learning L2 but not the other way round.	• L2 is 'bitty' and contains gaps; it is useful only for games really; therefore there is not enough L2 available to service L1. • I never want French to influence English. I never want to say: 'He ran away with all his legs'. • The L1 should be allowed to help the L2 and influence it to drop its structures in order to become a more natural, free flowing language. • My English is perfect and can't be helped, i.e. made better. My L2 is imperfect anyway, so how could it help my L1? • Knowledge of L1 can't even plug L2 gaps. So the opposite is impossible to imagine.

NB Two major differences in outlook on the value of a relationship between the L2 and the L1 are expressed below in the words of two individual learners who opposed each other in the debate:

Pupil A (G-I) In approbation of a relationship	Pupil B (G-E) In repudiation of a relationship
I do both French and German and I am amazed how French and English have things in common; German and English have things in common and French, German and English have things in common. I find this astounding! I see my own language in a totally different light and think about other cultures differently, too, knowing I would be able to relate with them, given the need and opportunity. Ideas are common to us all and there are many forms of language by which to share them!	The French and the Germans are different to us. Their cultures and languages and ideas are different. I don't expect to know their languages in order to communicate with them any more than I would need to understand and communicate in 'Mars' or 'Moon'. And no, they obviously do not affect my use of my own language.

The fourth questionnaire

This occurred during Easter 1992, on completing the work and assessment on *Tricolore 3* Unit 4 (the top and second sets – 4 sets – are involved) and explored the following issues:

1. how much time the pupils gave to French and/or German homework in a cycle of two weeks;
2. whether or not they revised for end-of-unit assessments;
3. and if 'yes', what exactly did they do?
4. whether they learned vocabulary;
5. what problems, if any, they had with the FL;
6. whether they would intentionally go absent from school in order to avoid
   – FL lessons
   – FL assessment
7. what things the teacher could do in order to make the teaching clearer;
8. what things the pupils could do in order to increase their learning and progress.

NB Since my questionnaires had become more demanding and the pupils' responses were also fuller, I had adopted a different method of charting the feedback, as shown in this and all subsequent instalments of the enquiry.

The responses to the fourth questionnaire

		G-I	%	G-E	%
1	Giving **no** time to homework	16/76	(21)	0/86	(0)
	Giving between 1 and 2 hours	41/76	(54)	78/86	(91)
	Giving as long as it takes	19/76	(25)	8/86	(9)
2	Showing a positive attitude to assessment	55/76	(72)	77/86	(90)
	Showing a negative attitude to assessment	21/76	(28)	9/86	(10)
3	Revision activities included:				
	– revision of structures and vocabulary	13/76	(17)	19/86	(22)
	– revision of course unit content	27/76	(35)	22/86	(26)
	– study of work in textbook and ex. bk	2/76	(3)	19/86	(22)
	– study of *sommaire* and special items	13/76	(17)	17/86	(20)
	– negative response, see above	21/76	(28)	9/86	(10)
4	Whether they learned vocabulary				
	– yes	35/76	(46)	40/86	(46.5)
	– no	21/76	(28)	6/86	(7)
	– sometimes/rarely	20/76	(26)	40/86	(46.5)
5	The FL-related problems were listed as:				
	– structures like verbs and tenses	21/76	(28)	28/86	(33)
	– skills like writing and speaking	17/76	(22)	28/86	(33)
	– topics like petrol stations	4/76	(5)	3/86	(3)
	– pace of lessons, difficulty of subject	12/76	(16)	9/86	(10)
	– problems with memory/vocabulary etc	10/76	(13)	11/86	(13)
	– problems of linking the language up	6/76	(8)	3/86	(3)
	– no, can't list them	6/76	(8)	4/86	(5)
6	On the possibility of absence from school to avoid FL lessons and assessment:				
	– lessons yes	10/76	(13)	8/86	(9)
	no	66/76	(87)	78/86	(91)
	– assessment yes	8/76	(11)	6/86	(7)
	no	68/76	(89)	80/86	(93)
	As the responses detailed here show, very few pupils admitted to a preparedness to go absent in MFL lessons and assessment. The reasons given by the few were **boredom**, **subject difficulty** and poor **results**.				

continued

	G-I	%	G-E	%
7 The following are responses to the questions of what the teacher could do to make lessons clearer:				
– slow down the pace of lesson delivery	16/76	(21)	25/86	(29)
– use more English, less French (FL)	12/76	(16)	6/86	(7)
– practise and vary the skills more regularly	9/76	(12)	13/86	(15)
– go over things more often and involve more worksheets	16/76	(21)	6/86	(7)
– explain the structures ('workings') more exhaustively, with more blackboard work	3/76	(4)	19/86	(22)
– acquire more subject time on the timetable	1/76	(1)	0/86	(0)
– no advice offered; don't know	10/76	(13)	13/86	(15)
– lessons satisfactory as they are now	9/76	(12)	4/86	(5)
8 To the inquiry about what the learners could do to increase their learning and extend their progress, the responses were:				
– don't know	4/76	(5)	7/86	(8)
– **ban the subject!**	2/76	(3)	2/86	(2)
– learn more things, more efficiently	5/76	(6)	18/86	(21)
– revise more often	36/76	(47)	27/86	(31)
– listen more, concentrate more, in class	19/76	(25)	27/86	(31)
– spend more time on the subject; do a little FL every night	7/76	(9)	5/86	(6)
– do regular, careful homework	1/76	(1)	0/86	(0)
– attend all lessons and be involved	4/76	(5)	0/86	(0)

THE FIFTH QUESTIONNAIRE

This occurred during Whitsun 1992, on completing the work and assessment on *Tricolore 3* Unit 5 (the two top sets only are reported here) and explored the following issues:

1. features of pupils' programmes of learning which they considered to be most important;
2. pupils' feelings about the use of the target language;
3. whether the use of the target language had made them more familiar with the foreign language;
4. whether they had made good progress with their courses;
5. aspects of study which they relied on repeating in Years 10 and 11;
6. whether they were ambitious to do well in the real GCSE;
7. the grade which they targeted ultimately.

The responses to the fifth questionnaire

		G-I	%	G-E	%
1	The most important features of the learning programmes were named as:				
	– topics: shopping for food	14/30	(47)	14/25	(56)
	don't know	16/30	(53)	9/25	(36)
	holidays	0/30	(0)	2/25	(8)
	– structures: tenses (time with verbs)	16/30	(53)	0/25	(0)
	don't know	14/30	(47)	24/25	(96)
	adjectives	0/30	(0)	1/25	(4)
2	On the pupils' feelings about the use of the target language, the responses were:				
	– OK, comfortable with it, accept it	17/30	(57)	11/25	(44)
	– would prefer more English	13/30	(43)	14/25	(56)
3	On whether TL use had brought familiarity with the foreign language:				
	– yes	22/30	(73)	18/25	(72)
	– no	8/30	(27)	7/25	(28)
4	On whether the pupils had made good progress with their courses:				
	– yes	15/30	(50)	25/25	(100)
	– no	1/30	(3)	0/25	(0)
	– don't know	14/30	(47)	0/25	(0)
5	On the aspects of study they would rely on repeating in the next two years:				
	– general structures	4/30	(13)	8/25	(32)
	– verbs and tenses	11/30	(37)	15/25	(60)
	– everything	4/30	(13)	1/25	(4)
	– don't know	7/30	(24)	1/25	(4)
	– the tests	1/30	(3)	0/25	(0)
	– certain topics	3/30	(10)	0/25	(0)
6	On whether they were ambitious to do well in the GCSE in Year 11:				
	– yes	24/30	(80)	25/25	(100)
	– no	4/30	(13)	0/25	(0)
	– not sure	2/30	(7)	0/25	(0)
7	On what grades they would target:				
	– C to A	28/30	(93)	23/25	(92)
	– Below C	2/30	(7)	2/25	(8)

80 — REFLECTIONS ON GRAMMAR-IMPLICIT LANGUAGE TEACHING

THE SIXTH QUESTIONNAIRE

This occurred during Christmas 1992, on completing the work and assessment on *Tricolore 4A* Units 1 and 2 – and on closing the first term of Year 10. (The language which now underpins the enquiry is exclusively French. The Two Sets One and the two Sets Two feature.) It explored the following issues:

1. what the learners understood by the terms 'grammar' and 'structures';
2. what language rules or knowledge they had learnt in connection with any language, including their own;
3. what special knowledge (implying grammar structures) they thought was needed in order to manage;
   - language in Speaking and Writing;
   - language in Listening and Reading;
4. whether they could list three areas of structural/grammatical difficulty or difference between French and English;
5. whether they were able to judge for themselves (implying instinctively) that what they said or wrote in English or in the foreign language was correct or incorrect;
6. whether they could explain on what grounds their spoken or written French would be correct or incorrect;
7. what they considered to be the most important aspect of their foreign language work;
8. whether they valued the fact that their FL lessons were delivered in the foreign language;
9. whether they had to think a thing out before they spoke it or wrote it;
10. what they considered the most reliably effective teaching tactics to be;
11. what they considered the most effective learning strategies to be;
12. whether they made conscious efforts to learn or whether learning was, for the most part, a natural and unconscious thing for them;
13. whether they had coped well with the revision/consolidation work, bridging Years 9 and 10;
14. whether they could do small grammar tasks:
    - make a simple question out of a statement;
    - re-write five phrases, applying adjectival agreements where necessary.

The responses to the sixth questionnaire

	G-I	%	G-E	%
1 On the ability to explain grammar or structures: – some satisfactory explanation given – no satisfactory explanation given	21/54 33/54	(39) (61)	29/44 15/44	(66) (34)
2 On the invitation to name some language rules, concerning any language: – citing verbs; tenses; adjectival agreements; gender; question-making; noun plurals; ' "i" before "e" except after "c" ' (in English); not starting a sentence with 'and' (in English); punctuation and pronunciation … – no examples offered	33/54 21/54	(61) (39)	38/44 6/44	(86) (14)

3 On the opinion whether grammar/rules and structures/special language knowledge … is needed in using language:
– in speech and writing: yes
                         no or don't know
– in listening and reading: yes
                            no or don't know
	35/54
	19/54
	30/54
	24/54
		(65)
		(35)
		(56)
		(44)
			42/44
			2/44
			31/44
			13/44
				(95)
				(5)
				(70)
				(30)

4 When invited to list three areas of structural difference or difficulty separating English and French: – affirmative responses, perceiving difficulties like: • the use of *avoir* where *être* is expected • the use of verbs as one word in the continuous situation • the lack of direct equivalents in the two languages • the importance of gender across the board • differences in word order, etc – negative responses (no differences perceived)	31/54 23/54	(57) (43)	38/44 6/44	(86) (14)
5 On whether they could judge their FL as correct or incorrect: – yes – no	29/54 25/54	(54) (46)	27/44 17/44	(61) (39)
6 On whether they could explain the criteria for judging language correctly: – yes – no	14/54 40/54	(26) (74)	25/44 19/44	(57) (43)

continued

		G-I	%	G-E	%
7	On naming the most important aspects of their FL work:				
	– structures	22/54	(41)	26/44	(59)
	– skills	11/54	(20)	14/44	(32)
	– mixed other	21/54	(39)	3/44	(7)
	– don't know or facetious other	0/54	(0)	1/44	(2)
8	On the value or not of teaching the FL (French) in the TL:				
	– yes	22/54	(41)	30/44	(68)
	– no	29/54	(54)	14/44	(32)
	– prefer half and half mixed of L1, L2	3/54	(5)	0/44	(0)
9	On whether they had to think an item out in L1 before speaking or writing it in L2:				
	– yes	33/54	(61)	38/44	(86)
	– no	10/54	(19)	1/44	(2)
	– don't know	11/54	(20)	5/44	(12)
10	On teaching strategies, numbers of learners who felt capable of naming specific, beneficial techniques:				
	– (could) yes	32/54	(59)	36/44	(82)
	– (could not) no	22/54	(41)	8/44	(18)
11	On learning strategies: numbers of learners who professed an awareness of effective measures:				
	– (could) yes	34/54	(63)	40/44	(91)
	– (could not) no	20/54	(37)	4/44	(9)
12	On whether they learned consciously or unconsciously:				
	– consciously	13/54	(24)	14/44	(32)
	– unconsciously	31/54	(57)	24/44	(54)
	– mixed, don't know	10/54	(19)	6/44	(14)
13	On whether they had remembered the consolidation work bridging Years 9 and 10:				
	– in whole or in part yes	25/54	(46)	23/44	(52)
	no	26/54	(48)	21/44	(48)
	– don't understand the reference	3/54	(6)	0/44	(0)
14	Concerning the responses on the grammar tasks set:				
	– pupils able to give responses	27/54	(50)	44/44	(100)
	– pupils unable to give responses	27/54	(50)	0/44	(0)

The responses of the action research learners — 83

THE SEVENTH QUESTIONNAIRE

This occurred in the Spring Term 1993 at the conclusion of Unit 3 of *Tricolore 4A*, and on closing the second term of Year 10. (Only the researcher's two top classes remain involved at this stage.) The pupils were asked in this instance to do the following things:

1. to name the tenses of verbs (or times) which were given in a list: *présent*; *passé*; *futur*;
2. to say whether they recognised the tenses easily or with difficulty now;
3. to say whether they could produce their verbs (action words) 'out of their heads' or whether they looked them up;
4. to say whether they had learnt a lot or only little about verbs and tenses (actions and times) so far;
5. to say whether they felt 'comfortable' or 'uncomfortable' about French at this stage of their studies.

The pupils' responses to the seventh questionnaire

		G-I	%	G-E	%
1	Ref. the first task of naming tenses; total number of correct responses	173/27 (av. 6.4)		165/25 (av. 6.6)	
2	Ref. whether they could now recognise the tenses: – yes – no	10/27 17/27	(37) (63)	10/25 15/25	(40) (60)
3	Ref. whether they worked their verbs out mentally before use or looked them up: – worked them out – looked them up	9/27 18/27	(33) (67)	6/25 19/25	(24) (76)
4	Ref. whether they had learnt much about verbs and tenses so far: – yes – no	20/27 7/27	(74) (26)	17/25 8/25	(68) (32)
5	Ref. whether they felt 'comfortable' about their French at that time: – yes – no	17/27 10/27	(63) (37)	10/25 15/25	(40) (60)

THE EIGHTH QUESTIONNAIRE

This occurred in the Summer Term 1993 at the conclusion of Units 4 and 5 of *Tricolore 4A*, and on closing the third term of Year 10. The pupils were asked for their responses to the following items:

1. whether they found the teaching method clear;
2. whether they could make any comment on this;
3. whether they would recommend changes in the teaching method;
4. whether they were making satisfactory progress in French;
5. what they thought it was that enabled this progress;
6. how much concentration they had, on a scale of 1 to 10;
7. what kind of memory they had.

The pupils' responses to the eighth questionnaire

		G-I	%	G-E	%
1	On whether they found the teaching methods clear:				
	– yes, clear	8/21	(38)	12/28	(43)
	– no, not clear	13/21	(62)	16/28	(57)
2	On whether they could comment on this:				
	– yes, able to	21/21	(100)	28/28	(100)
	– no unable to	0/21	(0)	0/28	(0)
3	On whether they would make changes in the teaching approach:				
	– yes	13/21	(62)	20/28	(71)
	– no	8/21	(38)	8/28	(29)
4	On whether satisfactory progress was being made:				
	– yes	11/21	(52)	14/28	(50)
	– no	10/21	(48)	14/28	(50)
5a	On whether the positive respondents understood what enabled this progress:				
	– yes	11/11	(100)	14/14	(100)
	– no	0/11	(0)	0/14	(0)
5b	On whether the negative respondents understood what impeded this progress:				
	– yes	10/10	(100)	14/14	(100)
	– no	0/10	(0)	0/14	(0)

continued

		G-I	%	G-E	%
6	On how much concentration they had on a scale of 1 to 10: – averages	117/21	(5.5)	148/28	(5.3)
7	On what kind of memory they had: – the most popular answer given by both classes G-I and G-E witnessed their own activities of 'writing' and 'reading' but also the teachers' use of visual aids	VISUAL

THE NINTH QUESTIONNAIRE

This occurred at the end of the academic year, July 1993, at the conclusion of Unit 5 of *Tricolore 4A* and on concluding the work of Year 10. The queries presented to the pupils were placed to investigate the following matters of interest:

1. which of the four skills best consolidated the learning;
2. whether they had good powers of recall;
3. whether they had a visual or an audio memory;
4. which skills they would prefer to increase their involvement with, if any;
5. whether they took sufficient responsibility for their own learning;
6. in the recent trial GCSE tests (end of Year 10 'Mocks') how their French results compared with those of the other subjects;
7. whether they found it easy to keep on working;
8. whether they were easily distracted;
9. what they would describe as the difficulties of being a teenage learner.

The pupils' responses to the ninth questionnaire

		G-I	%	G-E	%
1	On the skills favoured for consolidation of the learning: – active skills – passive skills	3/22 19/22	(14) (86)	1/26 25/26	(4) (96)
2	On their perceived powers of recall: – good – poor	4/22 18/22	(18) (82)	10/26 16/26	(38) (62)

continued

		G-I	%	G-E	%
3	On whether they had visual or audio memory:				
	– visual	15/22	(68)	23/26	(88)
	– audio	7/22	(32)	3/26	(12)
4	On which skills they might welcome more involvement with:				
	– active	8/22	(36)	3/26	(12)
	– passive	14/22	(64)	23/26	(88)
5	On taking sufficient responsibility for one's own learning:				
	– yes	6/22	(27)	8/26	(31)
	– no	16/22	(73)	18/2	(69)
6	On how French compared with the other subjects after testing:				
	– better	0/22	(0)	1/26	(4)
	– worse	13/22	(59)	20/26	(77)
	– the same	9/22	(41)	5/26	(19)
7	On how easily they keep on working:				
	– easy	6/22	(27)	2/26	(8)
	– hard	10/22	(46)	9/26	(34)
	– average	6/22	(27)	15/26	(58)
8	On whether they were easily distracted from their work:				
	– yes	18/22	(82)	21/26	(81)
	– no	4/22	(18)	5/26	(19)
9	On what it is like being a teenage learner under pressure:				
	– positive responses	1/22	(5)	10/26	(38)
	– negative responses	21/22	(95)	16/26	(62)

THE TENTH QUESTIONNAIRE

This occurred at the end of the Autumn/Winter term 1993, after the completion of Units 6 and 7 of *Tricolore 4B* and the Christmas 'Mock' GCSE examinations (the first questionnaire of Year 11). The questions which were put to the Year 11 pupils were as follows:

1. whether the 'Mocks' were easy, hard or half and half;
2. which paper pupils considered to be the hardest;
3. and which the easiest;

4. any valuable lessons which had been learnt from the experience of the 'Mocks';
5. whether they had got the results they wanted (expected, deserved);
6. whether they had got a good result or a poor result;
7. their plans at this stage for the real examination;
8. the grade which they targeted for the real examination;
9. which would now be more important for a successful outcome: the **teaching** or the **learning**;
10. which of the above two things has been most relied on so far: the **teaching** or the **learning**;
11. the points they would make in advising a friend on the best way to approach the GCSE course and examination in French.

The pupils' responses to the tenth questionnaire

		G-I	%	G-E	%
1	On how they found the 'Mocks': – easy – hard – half and half	 2/25 7/25 16/25	 (8) (28) (64)	 2/30 8/30 20/30	 (7) (27) (66)
2	On the perceived 'hardest' paper: – writing – reading – listening – speaking – equally/all	 12/25 1/25 8/25 3/25 1/25	 (48) (4) (32) (12) (4)	 1/30 0/30 16/30 3/30 10/30	 (3) (0) (53) (10) (34)
3	On the perceived 'easiest' paper: – writing – reading – listening – speaking – can't say/don't know	 1/25 16/25 2/25 5/25 1/25	 (4) (64) (8) (20) (4)	 5/30 21/30 2/30 2/30 0/30	 (16) (70) (7) (7) (0)
4	On the lessons learnt from the 'Mock' GCSE experience: – **revise** and **consolidate** the work – **no lessons learnt**	 23/25 2/25	 (92) (8)	 26/30 4/30	 (87) (13)

continued

	G-I	%	G-E	%
5,6 On how many of the pupils got the results:				
– wanted	11/25	(44)	21/30	(70)
– expected	17/25	(68)	8/30	(27)
– deserved	22/25	(88)	25/30	(83)
– good	15/25	(60)	20/30	(66)
– poor	10/25	(40)	8/30	(26)
7 On the plans made in preparation for the real GCSE:				
– more intensive revision	19/25	(76)	27/30	(90)
– other plans	5/25	(20)	0/30	(0)
– no plans	1/25	(4)	3/30	(10)
8 On what grades the pupils now targeted:				
– clear A	6/25	(24)	5/30	(17)
– above grade C	6/25	(24)	10/30	(33)
– happy with C	5/25	(20)	1/30	(3)
– borderline C/D	6/25	(24)	9/30	(30)
– below C/D	2/25	(8)	5/30	(17)
9,10 On whether they had so far relied on the teaching or the learning:				
– the **teaching**	18/25	(72)	16/30	(53)
– the **learning**	5/25	(20)	13/30	(43)
– both **equally**	2/25	(8)	1/30	(4)
NB results inverted with regard to revised intentions				
11 On the advice they would give to a friend doing GCSE French:				
– learn systematically and keep a positive attitude	24/25	(96)	28/30	(94)
– can't say	1/25	(4)	1/30	(3)
– don't take it	0/25	(0)	1/30	(3)

THE ELEVENTH QUESTIONNAIRE

This occurred at the start of the Whitsun break in the final teaching week, prior to 'the block release' and the onset of the GCSEs (May 1994). This final questionnaire explored the following issues:

1. the types of lessons which the pupils liked best;
2. the advice they would give to prospective GCSE pupils about:
   - their prospects for learning generally
   - their prospects for learning grammar specifically
   - their prospects for good results;
3. whether they felt confident about their GCSE examinations;
4. the revision processes which they intended to follow;
5. the changes which they would make to the teaching/learning styles if they had their time to do over again;

6. whether they would have preferred to be in the other set, giving reasons for their answers;
7. what they envisaged would be the hardest part of the examination for them (of the four skills);
8. and the hardest thing of all for them to do;
9. whether their awareness of grammar (or lack of it) would play a role in their performance and attainment;
10. what were they mostly concerned with when performing the skills;
11. their view as to the most important thing of all for the learners in the business of achieving a good outcome to the teaching and the learning;
12. whether they would do much revision for the actual French GCSE.

The pupils' responses to the eleventh questionnaire

		G-I	G-E
1	The most preferred lessons in order of preference were: 10 options in order of preference (1= top preference)		
	– group work	1	4
	– single skill: L R S W	4	2
	– didactic with much teacher talk	2=	3
	– pair work	7	1
	– teacher and blackboard	2=	5
	– mixture of everything	5	6=
	– worksheets	6	6=
	– heads down, writing	8	6=
	– mixed skills	10	9
	– other	9	10
2	On their advice to the new generation of GCSE French learners:		
	– go over the lesson later	✓	
	– don't waste time and opportunity	✓	
	– don't despair, you'll get used to things in time	✓	
	– **listen** and it's easier than you think	✓	✓
	– exposure to the target language trains you in using it	✓	
	– **blackboard** work clarifies things for you	✓	✓
	– keep motivated by learning as you proceed	✓	
	– you'll worry a lot; it's hard work		✓
	– you'll get fed up; it's boring		✓
	– avoid as much of it as you can; it's difficult		✓
	– engage with it and make notes	✓	✓
	– don't skip lessons	✓	✓
	– **concentrate**	✓	✓
	– stay off school		✓
	– give it up if you get the chance		✓

continued

		G-I	G-E
3	On their prospects for learning the subject generally: – make lots of notes always – hard work guarantees success – establish a sensible pace of work – accept your responsibilities to the work – there are very good prospects for workers – engage with the teacher – learn vocabulary and verbs as insurance – **concentrate** and **be willing** – everything's OK if you **listen** – FL involves **extra** work. Revise! – seek help if you need it	✓ ✓ ✓ ✓ ✓ ✓ ✓	 ✓ ✓ ✓ ✓ ✓ ✓ ✓
4	On learning the grammar: – it's vital to proper language use – try to figure it out but don't worry – you have good prospects for understanding it if you figure it out by examples – **listen hard** and you'll eventually get it – look out for features of the lessons – revise after lessons whenever you can – memorise the examples and build other examples on them – grammar is invisible therefore it must be a natural thing, an easy thing – grammar is hidden inside the vocabulary. If you learn the vocabulary, you must be learning the grammar – there's **lots of it**, so work at it! – it's hard work; difficult but possible – Ugh! No comment – bad stuff! Does your head in! – you have no choice but to learn it thoroughly. If you don't, you're doomed – it's the stuff that French has lots of – like mathematical and scientific formulae – and English doesn't have	✓ ✓ ✓ ✓ ✓ ✓ ✓ ✓ ✓ ✓	✓ ✓ ✓ ✓ ✓ ✓ ✓ ✓ ✓ ✓
5	On the prospects of getting good results in French: – good prospects if you **work** and **revise** – don't think ahead to results, you'll **panic** – simply work hard from **day to day** and the results will look after themselves – don't build your hopes up – your grade will reflect the effort you've made over time and it will be what you deserve – results mean opportunities	 ✓ ✓	✓ ✓ ✓ ✓

continued

		G-I	%	G-E	%
6	To the question about the state of the pupils' confidence in their anticipation of the GCSE examination in French:				
	– positive responses	16/23	(70)	16/27	(59)
	– negative responses	7/23	(30)	11/27	(41)
7	On what revision processes they would follow to this end:				
	– sundry positive responses	23/23	(100)	22/27	(81)
	– sundry negative responses	0/23	(0)	5/27	(19)
8	On the changes they would make (if they did the course again) to the teaching/learning business:				
	– (more explanation (slower pace (more use of English (more practice (increased, more intense, learning	14/23	(61)	15/27	(56)
	– no changes to the business	9/23	(39)	12/27	(44)
9	On whether and why (why not) they may have preferred to be in the other set!				
	– (it must be easier yes (a certain person is not there	3/23	(13)	9/27	(33)
	– (I like this set no (you learn more here (I would not like/I prefer the English component	20/23	(87)	18/27	(67)
10	On what the hardest part of the examination will be (1 is first choice etc):				
	– listening	2=		1	
	– reading	4		4	
	– speaking	2=		2	
	– writing	1		3	
11	On what was going to be the hardest thing of all for them to do (in rank order; 1 is hardest):				
	– listening	6		1=	
	– learning	3=		1=	
	– applying	3=		5	
	– recalling	3=		6=	
	– tense work	2		6=	
	– speaking	6=		4	
	– revision	1		1=	

continued

	G-I	%	G-E	%
12 On whether the awareness of grammar will play a role in their performance and attainment:				
– yes	16/23	(70)	15/27	(56)
– no	4/23	(17)	12/27	(44)
– can't say, don't know	3/23	(13)	0/27	(0)
13 On what they will be mostly concerned with in the exams:				
– vocabulary	13/23	(57)	14/27	(52)
– grammar	10/23	(43)	13/27	(48)
14 On defining the most important criteria for good achievement in order of priority: (1 is the highest priority out of 5 items cited)				
– motivation	1		1	
– self confidence	2		2	
– teaching styles	5		4=	
– learning strategies	4		3	
– completion of tasks	3		4=	

Comments on the overall enquiry into the learners' responses

The response to the final question of the final questionnaire is of considerable interest to the whole argument concerning teaching methods and their effects on learners. The matters of learners' states of **motivation** and **self-confidence** have repeatedly been found to be of paramount importance to successful outcomes for learners. **In any relevant discussion, the influence upon the learning process that these states produce may be considered as a vital part of the context of good classroom relationships with peers and teachers and to reach beyond the significance and value of a teaching style.**

The discussion of **motivation** and **self-confidence** is arguably an appropriate one to include here, since it displaces the temptation to make teaching styles or methods solely important to subject success for learners and then to make decisions on the (potential) superiority of particular teaching styles, notably in the AR between the teaching modes M1 and M2. All of this might be interpreted out of the perspectives of the G-I and G-E learners. Yet the learners' responses have given clear messages to confirm their understanding also of the importance of classroom relationships to their personal pursuit of a subject which has unique characteristics and which they found difficult. Such relationships with individual peer colleagues, whole peer units or settings and with subject teachers affect the learners' states of **motivation** and **self-confidence** (or, by analogy, have the power, conversely, to dismantle these).

The questionnaire inquiries and their returns suggest levels of interaction for teachers and for learners. These gain their energy from a number of psychological and methodological 'positives', such as the following:

- a **positive outlook**, a sense of interest and enthusiasm;
- a sense of **optimism**: the I **will**, I **can**, I **do** development;
- an awareness of **goals** and the **ambition** to achieve them;
- a **constructive approach** to the work and an **understanding of one's improving performance**;
- an acceptance of one's **personal responsibility** and **accountability** for the work and outcomes;
- a knowledge that **effective learning strategies** must be developed and activated; the issue of **revision** – the 'what' and the 'how' – was confronted as a matter to be addressed;
- an awareness of the importance of **participation, engagement, practice, concentration** and regular **consolidation** of the learning;
- an acceptance by the learner(s) of the teacher's guidance; full use of the teacher's knowledge and the **use of the teacher as principal resource** and as recourse, according to personal and collective need;
- an ability at all levels to work with peers as a means of **self-support** and reciprocal, informal **peer tutoring**, enabling an alternative method of **subject exploration** at an individual or small group level;
- an awareness of **the need to structure the links** which promote and improve the learning as the product of the subject experience, e.g. the **visual** link, always openly acknowledged by the AR learners, closely followed by the **audio** link;
- an acceptance that **the four language disciplines must be practised regularly** and meaningfully, per se and interactively, in order to maintain them and strengthen performance in the weaker areas;
- an understanding of the importance of training the facility of **recall**. Sometimes **active learning** has to be undertaken to a standard which improves the short-term and long-term **memory**. The principal subject for learning for recall purposes is **vocabulary**, which often embraces grammar matters also. To judge from certain of their responses, the AR learners

seemed to sense this, and the AR teachers relied upon this as a part of their efforts to address their teaching brief through M;

- an acknowledgement that **a foreign language is best taught and learnt through its own medium**. Used wholly and for all purposes, it carries its 'grammar' with it as a natural, uncontrived and unsequenced syllabus. The teacher can capture the best of all situations for the learner by accentuating the pedagogical grammar, which might merit specific attention, contained within the linguistic grammar. The **idiomatic** structures, which are a vital part of the FL's authentic characteristic, are floated to the learners in the most natural way and, on being gradually assimilated, they inform the learners' growing knowledge. They then enlarge their ability to comprehend the FL and to create material of their own in it. Accordingly they react more and more instinctively and appropriately to what is 'right' and 'wrong' in FL expression.

It is perhaps tempting to want to apply a more closely detailed analysis to the patterns that emerge from the data further to the general impressions which I have already listed above. Indeed, the findings have been more closely followed up by myself for my then current and later work. This is not the place for such an exhaustive screening of the characteristics of the questionnaires, however. Nevertheless, one or two points quite obstinately stand out, e.g.:

- the stronger reaction of the G-E class to 'grammar', throughout and especially in the Year 11 inquiries;
- the increasing acknowledgment of both classes of the place and importance of the target language to MFL practice;
- the repeated suggestions that the G-E class in general worried about the subject more than its twin;
- the mutual preoccupation with 'verbs and tenses' and the admission that both classes of learners made to looking them up. (There was little actual evidence of this. If only!);
- the evidence that both classes were aware of their poor memory capacity and, relevantly, emphasised the importance of the **visual** appeal made through the use of AV aids (and 'action' agendas);
- the fact that both classes confessed to a reliance upon the teacher prior to their systematic recognition that their own effort counted much more;
- the development that by Year 11 (and, significantly, in the light of the AR), **listening** was declared as the most difficult language discipline by the G-E learners as opposed to **writing** in the case of Set One (G-I). And so on.

These questionnaires and their relevant responses were not the full complement of the inquiries that I staged with my classes. They have been selected as the most suitable to furnish this report. There were others, more individual and more focused, as the process became ongoing. What they reveal of the differences and similarities between the AR parallel groups is self-evident as the questionnaires are read. For the purpose of this book, it is perhaps not inappropriate to leave this area of the investigation as an open field of information for readers to explore.

The more it becomes clear that the world of the foreign language learner and that of the subject teacher overlap and occupy common ground in more terms than merely the classroom and the syllabus that they share, the closer we come to being able to put a sensible perspective on the vexed issue of FL teaching method and the importance to it of 'grammar teaching'. In this account I have depicted the responses of teachers and learners to the classroom business which they shared during that spotlighted period of time. However, the feedback generated the insight that, in the usual course of events, these voices too often remained divided and neglected to interact.

Clearly, **teaching** does not equal **learning**, but neither concept can stand alone without the other. As a result of my AR experience, I feel strongly that the best teaching is done by teachers who use methods, approaches and personal styles that are informed with a knowledge of the expected and actual patterns of psychological development relevant to the learners they are involved with and responsible for. Such an awareness implies a respect for their cognitive, social and maturity statuses, their physical, physiological, emotional and conceptual levels of growth as youngsters at specific ages. Their ability ranges, year groups, class settings, their identities as individual human beings and as indigenous youth of the geographic, social and economic areas into which they were born must be taken into consideration also. This is clearly a huge responsibility for teachers: to be **sensitive**, **sympathetic**, **empathetic** and **cognisant**. Yet we can be and we must be these things. On a daily basis we are immersed in the physical and emotional world of young people. Our training in part, our gathering experience as concerned and inquiring practitioners, our roles as pastoral tutors and our natural aptitudes for working with the young, enable us to meet mind with mind in an effective and productive way. As always, reading on educational psychology helps.

Having gone through the protracted procedure of my action research I have found myself standing in the middle of an equation which affects us all in National Curriculum times. The raw results attained by the learners in the course of their AR work to GCSE are revealed in the chapter which follows. There it will be seen whether or not 'grammar-implicit' teaching, in the manner in which I have interpreted it and activated it in my own department's context, found a vacuum in which to fall or fulfilled the expectations that the NC in Modern Foreign Languages has invested in it.

Chapter 7

The subject outcomes attained by the action research learners

Evaluating the action research through the performances of the learners

The results which this chapter aims to present are the outcomes of two kinds of performance made by the learners in my action research. In the first place, they reflect the participants' **skills performances**, measured characteristically in marks and ultimately in GCSE grades. In the second place, their **grammatical competence** is measured in terms of mark scores awarded as a means of counting synchronous grammar use, grammar recognition and the correct manipulation of grammar practised in mechanical exercises. The patterns which are seen to emerge have provided the information, i.e. the evidence I have sought for a better understanding of the much debated issue of foreign language teaching and the relationship to this of a defined grammar-syllabus.

The long journey through the action research had produced interim results from work and tests which had been done in stages. These results were written up in the same stages as they emerged. The patterns of the performances of the G-E and G-I groups fluctuated and changed continually, as each side of the experiment pursued its own path, and within the development of their contrastive study as they competed with each other. Because of the long duration of the AR and the natural vicissitudes that so much time inevitably generates, I was prevented from discerning regular patterns of evolvement in the learners' performances. In addition, the AR work was influenced and affected by the changes that time brought to the learners' general state of maturation, specifically their psychological, cognitive, emotional and physical development. I knew the AR learners very well, having worked with them in a more than ordinary and more than ordinarily intense relationship for so long. Even so, it was not until the last set of data was committed to the results-appraisal process that I was able to venture a judgment on what had evolved.

I had entered the contrastive study of teaching methods with an open mind. However, whenever I was pressed to give my personal view on which of my two trialled methods would emerge as the more effective, I chose M2, confident of the power of the factor X, having done my own learning and my teaching hitherto under its influence, to one degree or another. It promised to be an interesting exercise, observing the patterns leading up to the final analysis and the actual disclosure of the AR's more effective teaching mode.

It is not my intention to incorporate in any real detail the 'mathematics' or research methods which produced the results to which I allude in this chapter. The sections which follow will selectively but representatively focus upon the developments that the maths identified on behalf of the groups G-I and G-E separately and in (undeclared) competitive association with each other.

The results in Year 9

By the end of Year 9 the performance of the whole year group could be appraised on the following lines:

- featuring the two half-year 'factions', G-I and G-E competitively;

- in the contexts of the four language skills (or Attainment Targets) of Listening, Reading, Writing, Speaking;

- across the spectrum of six half-termly assessment tests, comprising five from the *Tricolore 3* assessment-system and concluding with the 1987 past NEAB/GCSE paper at Basic Level;

- noting an end-of-year appraisal of regular German assessments attesting to the whole year's work in this second foreign language.

In terms of the comprehensive assessment, the factions' results were measured as almost equal:

- almost equal when all sets and two languages were involved;

- almost equal when only French was measured;

- identical when only German was measured.

That is not, however, to say that the parallel settings gained identical results, or that there was a consistent pattern of 'superiority' throughout. That certainly was not the case, as the following simple diagram shows, in allowing the symbol ✓ to denote the acquisition of a superior score:

98 — REFLECTIONS ON GRAMMAR-IMPLICIT LANGUAGE TEACHING

Assessment No.	Listening G-I G-E	Reading G-I G-E	Speaking G-I G-E	Writing G-I G-E	German G-I G-E	Combined G-I G-E
1	✓ ✓		= =	✓	✓	2x ✓ 2x ✓
2	✓ ✓		✓	= =	✓	4x ✓ 0x ✓
3	✓	✓	✓	✓	✓	2x ✓ 3x ✓
4	✓	✓	= =	= =	✓	0x ✓ 3x ✓
5	✓	✓	= =	= =	✓	1x ✓ 2x ✓
6	✓ ✓		= =	✓	✓	3x ✓ 1x ✓
	3x✓ 3x✓	3x✓ 3x✓	1x✓ 1x✓	2x✓ 1x✓	3x✓ 3x✓	12x✓ 11x✓

In the case of the **full year group**, divided into its two competing half-factions, the general progress curves could be depicted in their different characteristics as follows:

Superior gains

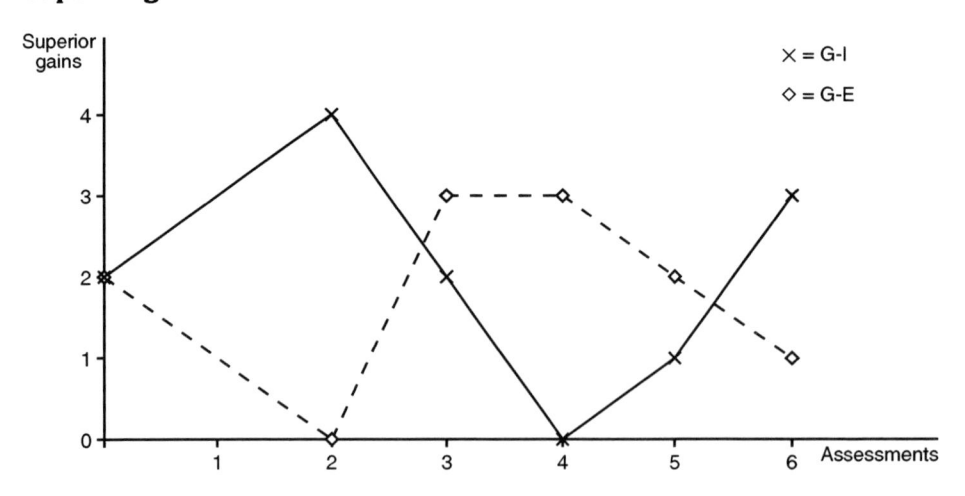

Of the further patterns which emerged from the Year 9 assessment processes, the following were of interest:

1. **Concerning the two Sets Two in French**, the G-E set emerged apparently more than twice as strong as its G-I counterpart. Much speculation could be invested into accounting for this difference, especially since the story of their experience of M has already been told through their teachers' reflections. However, because of the indeterminate nature of the teachers' and groups' passage with M, and since the two groups were shortly afterwards to discontinue their participation in the AR, I prefer to leave such speculation untapped at this juncture.

2. **Concerning the two Sets Four in French**, the G-I set was apparently more extrovert, therefore seemed sharper, cleverer, keener and more able than the G-E set to take the rigours of the methodological experiment. In the context of the Listening and Reading assessments the Set Four (G-I) obtained marks which seemed to challenge those of the top sets, whereas the performance of the Set Four (G-E) tended to reflect its status as a typical Set Four by comparison. The comprehension marks from the first three assessments reflect this pattern (and suggest possible speculation on this area of MFL pursuit for another occasion, one might say):

Assessments		Set One G-I	Set Two G-I	Set Four G-I	Set One G-E	Set Two G-E	Set Four G-E
One	Listening/25	12.7	11.0	12.4	14.1	11.3	8.9
	Reading/25	9.8	11.1	10.0	14.8	10.7	5.4
Two	Listening/25	16.7	13.2	14.4	16.3	13.5	10.2
	Reading/25	17.8	10.8	13.9	15.9	12.4	6.8
Three etc	Listening/25	13.6	12.4	11.8	13.8	10.2	10.4
	Reading/25	16.1	11.4	16.0	18.0	12.3	8.1

3. **Concerning the performances in German of the two top sets G-I and G-E**: these generated a 'swings-and-roundabouts' pattern, which contained the same initial down-scale but inverse fluctuations latterly. They averaged out almost equally, in the end, or conceded a small advantage to G-E. Only the end-of-unit (combined-skills) assessment results are applied here:

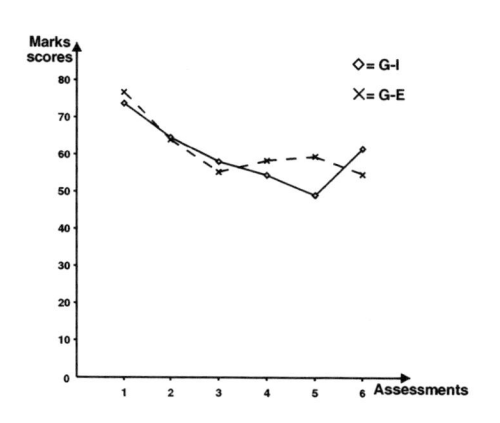

	G-I (%)	G-E (%)
1st assessment	73.7	76.7
2nd assessment	64.6	64.0
3rd asssssment	58.0	55.2
4th assessment	54.4	58.3
5th assessment	49.0	59.7
6th assessment	61.5	54.6
Combined average	60.2	61.4

100 — REFLECTIONS ON GRAMMAR-IMPLICIT LANGUAGE TEACHING

4. **Concerning the performances of the two Sets One in French**, the whole assessments disclosed an acutely run race, with the final outcome establishing the G-I top set's advantage by a five-mark margin. (NB whole assessment = combined skills).

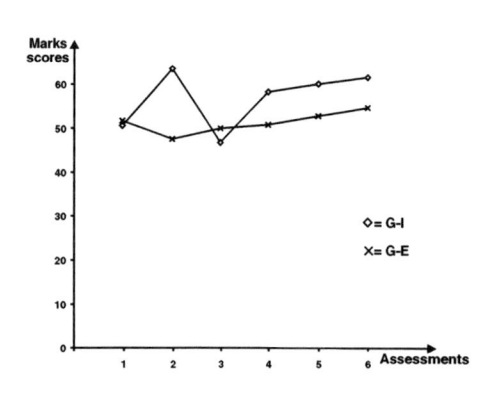

	G-I (%)	G-E (%)
1st assessment	50.6	51.7
2nd assessment	63.5	47.6
3rd asssment	46.8	50.0
4th assessment	58.2	50.8
5th assessment	60.0	52.8
6th assessment	61.5	54.6
Combined average	56.7	51.3

5. **Concerning the grammar-focused performances of the two Sets One in Year 9**, only a general sounding was taken of the learners' emerging grammatical awareness. The evidence which I obtained was based on: (i) the overall impressions of some application of grammar and (ii) a number of actual grammar counts undertaken in skills' practice and mechanical exercises at later stages of the year's work. The simple pattern placed below depicts the outcome of this first tentative inquiry (3 indicates superior awareness and use):

	Set One (G-I)	Set One (G-E)	Total in G-I	G-E
Assessment 1		Perfect tense ✓	2x ✓	4x ✓
Assessment 2	Future tense ✓			
Assessment 3		Tenses combined ✓		
Assessment 4	Pronouns =	Pronouns= Adjectives ✓		
Assessment 5	Imperfect ✓			
GCSE 1987	Perfect =	Perfect = Adjectives ✓		

Notes of comment on the performances of the Sets One

The charts and graphs which have been offered for German and for French are intended to incite speculation about these two sets of learners whose job it was to learn their foreign languages by partly similar, partly opposing methods. The information given may witness the effects of the methods upon the learners and/or the characteristic of their group's temperament, ability and aptitude and the stamp that certain individuals placed upon this in order to disrupt it and cause further fluctuations. In addition, there are factors like levels of motivation, truancy and absence from school which prejudice performance. My close observations of the Sets One during the first year of French in the High School persuaded me that the pupils were fairly well motivated and not without optimism and self-confidence in relation to the informed 'character reference' which I gave the year group on introducing them in Chapter 3. There was no history of truancy from French lessons in particular, but their school attendance records became erratic as time went by. In view of our concern about the year group's outlook and relationship with its education, we AR teachers later read with interest OFSTED's (1995 PICSI) warning on the effect on academic performance of absenteeism.

The results in Year 10

In this section and the next, the commentary will focus on the performances of the two Sets One, learning French, since all the other group components of the AR had by this time terminated their participation in it or would soon do so. In Year 10 the principal assessment was structured at end-of-term intervals. For the purposes of the AR, it was given the form of past NEAB/GCSE papers at Basic Level on the first two testing occasions, and at both Basic and Higher Level in the summer of 1993, concluding the Year 10 work. The relevant results table, attached to this section, identifies (through the use of the symbol 3) the superior performance of the G-I set. In addition, however, there is evidence of the G-E set's better performance in the single skill of 'Writing'. This was a development from the Year 9 situation, in which the G-E group had produced a better result in the 'Reading' skill (not shown in the tables used in that section of this chapter).

Grammar

At the end of Year 10, I assessed the two groups' production of grammar over the year, by consulting my grammar log of marks for accuracy of application and points indicating instances of appropriate grammar use. It became clear that at this stage the G-I learners had attained higher marks in the majority of the mechanical exercises that I had included in the agenda, whereas the G-E learners had produced more frequently occurring, accurate application of grammar when this was an integral part of their skills-work. (I admit to finding this outcome quite ironic, since I would have anticipated the opposite to occur!) When these separate grammatical performances were united, however, the groups' respective scores

REFLECTIONS ON GRAMMAR-IMPLICIT LANGUAGE TEACHING

TWO TOP SETS: YEAR 10 ASSESSMENT IN FRENCH
Three principal tests, using past papers in GCSE (BL = basic level; HL = higher level)

SKILL		Set One (G-I)				No of ✓	3 assessments combined	No of ✓		Set One (G-E)			SKILL
		GSCE BL 1992	GSCE BL 1991	GSCE BL/HL 1989	3 assessments combined				GSCE BL/HL 1989	GSCE BL 1991	GSCE BL 1992	
Listening: Av.		10.5 ↘	16.7 ↘	14.2 ↘	13.8 ↘	(4)	11.3		13.0	11.2	9.8	Av.: Listening
SD		3.93	3.17	5.57	4.22		3.96		4.36	3.80	3.73	SD
Reading: Av.		12.5	15.5 ↘	26.6 ↘	18.2 ↘	(3)	16.0	(1)	21.6	13.3	13.3 ↘	Av.: Reading
SD		3.97	3.22	8.38	5.19		3.41		4.81	3.18	2.97	SD
Speaking: Av.		14.1 ↘	11.4	17.7 ↘	14.4 ↘	(3)	14.1	(1)	16.3	12.7 ↘	13.4	Av.:Speaking
SD		5.02	4.72	9.28	6.34		6.12		7.87	4.78	5.71	SD
Writing: Av.		15.7	9.7	25.8 ↘	17.0	(1)	17.2 ↘	(3)	24.1	11.0 ↘	16.7 ↘	Av.: Writing
SD		4.14	4.91	11.38	6.81		6.1		9.45	4.16	4.67	SD
Whole (%) Av. performance		48.2	53.0 ↘	45.8 ↘	49.0	(3)	46.5	(1)	40.9	48.3	50.4 ↘	Av. (%) whole performance
SD		22.30	13.23	33.5	23.01		18.85		24.25	14.56	17.76	SD
Scores by ✓						(14)		(6)				Scores by ✓

combined to produce **equal** marks-totals in collective grammar competence. When the two issues of general language performance and grammar competence were integrated, the G-I Set One emerged as the stronger of the two groups.

Clearly, a number of shifts had taken place in the two top sets' FL development since the beginning of their course in Year 9. Equally clearly, there was the potential for further shifts to occur as the pupils' work moved into the final phase of the GCSE course and the concluding phase of the action research.

The results in Year 11

PART 1 – FORMAL ASSESSMENTS

The assessments detailed here were delivered through past GCSE examination papers (NEAB) at both Basic and Higher Levels. The occurrence of the year group's real GCSE examination in the Summer term of this final year implies that this was a short academic year from point of view of classroom activity. This in itself placed time constraints on the remaining subject agenda and limited the opportunities for testing, at a time when the teaching and learning process was assuming the paramount importance. Even so, the two full assessments which were carried out during this year acted as trial examinations (the 1993 examination featuring at the time of the school's official Year 11 'Mocks'). This enabled a diagnostic appreciation of the pupils' individual situations in the subject as well as providing late-stage and crucial information for the purposes of my action research.

Where my methodological experiment was concerned, the assessments were considered as usual as a comparative appraisal of the two Sets One and the 'superior' results were again indicated by means of ✓ and counted. In a similar way, the closer standard deviation (SD) readings were identified through the placing of asterisks (*).

It is clear that the top sets' GCSE trialling experience brought interesting results at three levels of observation:

1. at the level of the individual skills, in which case 'superior' performances have been indicated (by the symbol ✓), no matter how small the difference between the competing scores;

2. at the level of the standard deviation readings, since these reflected information regarding the composition and characteristics of the two groups (e.g. homogeneity and heterogeneity). This enlarged on the statements made by the average scores;

3. at the level of the average scores. It became clear that the two groups' performances were very closely matched.

104 — REFLECTIONS ON GRAMMAR-IMPLICIT LANGUAGE TEACHING

		G-I	GCSE 1992		GCSE 1993 Set One		Combined			Combined		GCSE 1993 Set One		GCSE 1992 (G-E)	
Listening	AV SD	(/32)	11.6 4.41	✓	(/71)	30.8 9.80	(/55)	21.2 7.10	✓	(/55)	19.6 4.84*	(/71)	28.7 6.44*		10.5 3.24*	(/32)	Listening AV SD
Reading	AV SD	(/48)	22.3 7.35	✓	(/78)	39.1 11.83	(/63)	30.7 9.59		(/63)	29.4 8.11*	(/78)	39.6 10.30*		19.2 5.92*	(/48)	Reading AV SD
Speaking	AV SD	(/40)	23.2 6.00		(/66)	40.7 14.44	(/53)	31.9 10.22	✓or=	(/53)	32.6 7.63*	(/66)	40.8 10.63*	✓	24.4 4.64*	(/40)	Speaking AV SD
Writing	AD SD	(/64)	34.0 9.79*	✓	(/60)	30.0 10.43	(/62)	32.0 10.11*	✓	(/62)	34.5 10.94	(/60)	32.1 7.93*	✓	37.0 13.95	(/64)	Writing AV SD
Whole performance	AV SD	(%)	49.5 20.48*	=	(%)	50.9 43.90	(%)	50.2 32.19	✓	(%)	50.4 26.13*	(%)	51.3 30.17*	=	49.5 22.10	(%)	Whole performance AV SD
MID	AV	(%)	48.7	✓	(%)	47.5	(%)	48.1	✓	(%)	49.0	(%)	50.6		47.8	(%)	MID AV
MID	SD		11.27			25.83		18.55			10.04*		11.67*		8.41*		MID SD
Ticks				3✓		1✓ (G-I) 6x ✓		2✓	4✓		5* 11x ✓		6* 5 ✓(G-E)	2✓			Ticks
Closer SD			2*			(G-I) 3*		1*					15* (G-E)		4*		Closer SD

In whole-performance terms the groups are almost identical at this stage and it is left to the small differences in the separate skills areas to allow a contrived advantage to be placed with the G-E group this time.

PART 2 – MISCELLANEOUS WORK

The following is a representative record of Year 11 marks depicted as whole group averages. They pertain to classwork and homework performed in the four language skills and selected according to two conditions: (i) that there was an attendance of 28 pupils in each case and (ii) that the mark list contained a distribution of marks which reflected the groups' various ability ranges as the outcomes of exercises which had implied differentiation appropriately (hence the few instances selected for Reading and Speaking):

Listening			Reading			Speaking			Writing		
Out of	G-I	G-E	Out of	G-I	G-E	Out of	G-I	G-E	Out of	G-I	G-E
46	35.6 ✓	34.8	20	16.5 ✓	14.6	60	45.5 ✓	42.3	30	14.8	15.2 ✓
17	8.1	9.5 ✓	36	31.7 ✓	30.3	50	39.1 ✓	36.5	30	24.2 ✓	22.0
25	13.5	16.0 ✓	51	34.8 ✓	31.7	25	21.6	21.6	40	28.8 ✓	27.4
14	7.8	8.2 ✓	27	22.7 ✓	22.2	50	34.3 ✓	26.2	100	64.5 ✓	61.4
26	10.6	10.6				30	20.7 ✓	15.8	60	35.8	38.0 ✓
15	10.7	12.6 ✓				34	25.6 ✓	19.5	25	18.0 ✓	16.4
30	12.3	16.0 ✓				34	20.1 ✓	17.8	60	49.0 ✓	40.9
70	43.8 ✓	39.5							25	18.5 ✓	17.1
40	21.6	23.0 ✓							50	33.2 ✓	27.7
18	15.1 ✓	14.3							50	37.5 ✓	20.9
70	41.7 ✓	38.8									
30	17.0 ✓	15.0									
30	20.1 ✓	19.5									
30	13.2 ✓	12.5									
28	12.3	14.2 ✓									
60	28.4	31.9 ✓									
av 34.3	19.3	19.9 ✓	av 33.4	26.6 ✓	24.9	av 40.4	29.7 ✓	25.6	av 47.0	32.4 ✓	28.7
count in ✓	7 ✓	9 ✓		5 ✓	0 ✓		7 ✓	0 ✓		9 ✓	2 ✓

Superiority of performance measured in ✓ (complete)	G-I	28 ✓		G-E	11 ✓
Superiority of performance measured in skills averages / 4	G-I	3 skills (R,S,W)		G-E	1 skill (L)

Just as it could be argued from the evidence contained in this scores-chart, that the G-I Set One learners tended to put on a better around-the-year show than the G-E group, there was evidence also of a more positive and competent application of grammar structures on their part. Of fifteen grammar matters observed comparatively, the G-I Set One addressed nine of them with better understanding than its G-E twin. In the remaining six matters the groups' performances were equal or almost equal.

Summary

The patterns which have emerged in the three results-analyses outlined on behalf of the Sets One (G-I and G-E) over three years prior to their GCSE in French in the Summer of 1994 are:

In Year 9	Set One (G-I) performed better in general use of the language
	Set One (G-E) performed better at grammar
In Year 10	Set One (G-I) performed better in general use of the language
	The two sets performed equally at grammar
In Year 11	The Set One (G-E) performed arguably better in general use of the language
(pre-GCSE '94)	The Set One (G-I) performed arguably better at grammar

The results of the 1994 GCSE examination in French

At the outset I believed that this final stage in the design of my action research would be discussed in terms of rather general findings. However, thanks to the generosity of the NEAB, I was given access to my pupils' test papers and 'Speaking' tapes for the length of time it took me to extract and log the detailed information I required on (i) their language performance in the four skills and (ii) the competence they showed in comprehending and applying the grammar structures which were the in-built agenda.

Considering first the matter of expressed grammatical competence, I was able to demonstrate through my system of counting grammar uses across the GCSE papers and orals, that the Set One (G-I) emerged as the more competent group of the two. This 'superiority', however, was a technical one only, since the differences in the groups' grammar scores were as small as those which have been demonstrated as samples earlier in this chapter. Yet before settling down to deciding that these grammar counts proved a case of no significant difference in the performances and competences of my two groups, I stopped to consider that, however small, **they were real**, and they had been acquired by one of the two sets, namely G-I.

Considering secondly the actual GCSE examination results, it became clear that the NEAB had advised an average grade D award for each of the two Sets One.

The G-I class gained its average grade at a point within the defined 'D' category and the G-E class fell below this marker by arguably a ¼ grade. Again, therefore, one can claim that there was no statistically significant difference between the performances of the groups. When Levene's Test for Equality of Variances was applied, that was, indeed, the very decision which was seen to emerge, and it applied to **all** of the examinations: the four skills tests separately and the whole examination at Basic and Higher levels, combining all the components. I had no problem accepting the scientific argument, but once again I reflected that, as in the case of the small grammar margins, there was here also a small but nevertheless real margin of difference, of 'superiority', and it occurred on the side of the G-I setting! Furthermore, the grades-patterns which produced the near-same grade D averages were interesting to observe. The table which follows establishes the Set One (G-I) as the keeper of the higher status awards. In the light of the SD patterns (and their messages concerning the relative homogenous nature of each teaching group) which have been indicated in this chapter, this model or similar might have been expected, it might be argued. Even so, it made an interesting exercise to chart the grades from the point of view of the dispersal or spread patterns which emerged for the two groups:

	Number of examinees attaining grades	
Grade	Set One (G-I) / 28	Set One (G-E) / 29
A*	0	0
A	3	0
B	4	1
C	5	10
D (average)	5	8
E	8	7
F	3	3
G	0	0
U	0	0
Average grade	D	D
	greater grades – spread	smaller grades – spread

An inspector's judgment in comparing the groups' results might be based on raw percentages of class numbers occurring above the Grade C bench mark: 43% in the case of G-I and 38% in the instance of G-E.

In order to find out more about the potential significance of this grades-pattern, I plotted the two sets' French results in a chart carrying also their GCSE grades-results for the four core subjects: English Language, English Literature, Maths and Science. Within the chart (see p.109) it will be seen that against each grade a number has been placed to act as a value for the grade. This device helped in the process of calculating average grades in those subject contexts that were being used in this comparative exercise. The number values in question are:

A*8   A7   B6   C5   D4   E3   F2   G1   U0.

Reflections on the outcomes of the AR and its impact on the learners and their performances

In the light of the comparative five-subject table which follows, the concluding reflections on the potential effectiveness of grammar-implicit teaching (M), as this was designed and trialled in my AR, may be articulated as follows:

The Set One (G-E) had established a general grades-superiority over the Set One (G-I), systematically: ie in four out of the five analysed subjects by averages-margins ranging from 0.2 to 0.9 (i.e. a fraction of a grade to a whole grade). It had lost this relative predominance to Set One (G-I) in French, however, as well as also having clearly ceded the higher status grades-results to this group. I have noted this possible positive correlation between this group's work and the M1 (or G-I) teaching mode applied on its behalf. Most certainly **the absence of the factor X** in its designed format seems not to have harmed its pupils' performance in French. More significantly, perhaps, **the presence of the factor X** in the work of the G-E group appears to have offered those learners **no advantage** over their G-I peers in either of the two contexts examined in my action research: (i) general French language performance as demonstrated in their work in the four skills; (ii) competence displayed as awareness and application of French grammar as evinced in all the aspects of their work.

The results emerging from the action research have been looked at from a number of perspectives, including those charted in this chapter. I feel that the final honest conclusion to this action research story may be placed with confidence in the superiority of the G-I group's results over those of its G-E twin group in the French GCSE examinations of 1994. In this local experiment, therefore, the case for grammar-implicit MFL teaching at this level of study had been substantiated. The explicit grammar summaries appeared to add little for many and to confuse some. Despite the inevitable variables and imponderables which my AR encountered, despite the small margins of difference which occurred in the calculations, and despite other considerations which might be taken into account, I feel I dare make this claim.

My concluding comments on the insights gained from the outcomes of the action research programme are given in the next and final chapter of this book.

The subject outcomes attained by the AR learners — 109

Set One G-I	French	English language	English literature	Maths	Science	Set One G-E	French	English language	English literature	Maths	Science
1	D4	C5	B6	C5	D4		C5	A7	A7	A7	C5
2	A7	B6	B6	A7	D4		E3	C5	B6	C5	D4
3	E3	C5	D4	A7	C5		C5	B6	B6	A7	A7
4	D4	D4	D4	C5	C5		E3	B6	B6	B6	C5
5	F2	B6	B6	C5	B6		E3	B6	B6	A*8	B6
6	E3	C5	B6	D4	D4		F2	D4	C5	C5	D4
7	D4	C5	C5	B6	D4		E3	B6	B6	B6	D4
8	B6	A7	A7	A*8	A*8		C5	A7	A7	A7	B6
9	B6	B6	B6	A7	B6		F2	B6	C5	C5	D4
10	E3	B6	A7	C5	B6		F2	B6	B6	A*8	A7
11	A7	A7	A7	A7	B6		E3	B6	B6	C5	D4
12	E3	E3	E3	Abs	F2		B6	A7	A7	B6	D4
13	E3	D4	C5	D4	E3		D4	C5	C5	A7	D4
14	E3	B6	A7	D4	U0		D4	B6	B6	C5	C5
15	D4	C5	C5	D4	C5		C5	A7	A7	B6	B6
16	B6	B6	B6	C5	D4		D4	B6	B6	A7	E3
17	B6	B6	B6	A7	A7		C5	B6	B6	C5	E3
18	E3	C5	B6	E3	E3		D4	D4	D4	E3	E3
19	D4	A7	A7	B6	C5		D4	C5	C5	C5	B6
20	F2	D4	D4	D4	D4		C5	B6	B6	A7	B6
21	A7	B6	A7	B6	C5		C5	B6	B6	A*8	A7
22	C5	B6	A7	B6	B6		E3	C5	C5	A7	C5
23	C5	C5	D4	B6	D4		C5	C5	C5	C5	B6
24	F2	D4	E3	E3	F2		D4	B6	B6	F2	E3
25	C5	C5	B6	C5	D4		C5	C5	B6	B6	B6
26	C5	B6	A7	D4	D4		D4	C5	B6	C5	C5
27	C5	C5	B6	D4	C5		D4	B6	C5	A*8	A7
28	E3	E3	E3	B6	D4		E3	C5	C5	A7	C5
29							C5	B6	B6	A7	D4
Total points	120	148	156	143	125		115	166	168	175	144
Av. points	4.28	5.28	5.57	5.10	4.46	3.96	5.72	5.79	6.03	4.96	
Grade from points		D	C	C	C	D		D	C	C	B	C
↑ = superior grade		↑						↑	↑	↑	↑	
Points-based SD		1.56	1.08	1.34	1.35*	1.62		1.08*	0.79*	0.72*	1.45	1.29*

Chapter 8

Evaluating the grammar-implicit (G-I) principle

The conditions needed for the appropriate delivery of the G-I teaching mode

My action research in the G-I teaching of GCSE French, as a process and in its results, has indicated that, at that specific level of occupation, **an explicit grammatical agenda in native language delivery is not imperative to the teaching of a modern foreign language when the target language is fully employed in the teaching/learning process**. Having set out to test the National Curriculum's hypotheses on MFL teaching methods, I seem to have emerged from my own particular trials proving them viable. To an extent, I feel that my work echoes in the practical sense what e.g. Mitchell and Rivers have been writing for some time on the subject of communicative teaching and learning and what the latter wrote in her 1990 publication:

> 'The continual use of language in interaction with others is basic to successful learning and teaching. For effective language learning in the classroom, we need an interactive approach, where emphasis is placed on the whole fabric of language …' (p.v)

Thus the writers' target is to bring the teaching together with the learning, which makes obvious, good sense in terms of today's **communicative approach**. Then the aim is to hone the concept of this approach into an essentially shared interactive/communicative classroom process. Without a doubt, if this development is not made, the most efficacious situation for learners will not necessarily be found in this G-I teaching approach. Meanwhile, teachers gain only frustration for their efforts and learners risk getting confused and too often left behind in too much ignorance of the subject. Learners must **talk**, i.e. communicate in the foreign language with their teacher and with each other. The former happens little, the latter even less, if at all. The NC Programme of Study (January 1995) has expressed its ambition that our classroom business in MFL should practise a number of principles that it preaches on the subject of the teaching method just discussed:

- learning the target language through using it;
- combining and integrating the language skills;
- facilitating interactive communication in a variety of activities;
- considering, wherever possible, that the hierarchical grading and sequencing of content is not relevant to the TL agenda.

Having already referenced Heafford on the losses implied in the use of a method which keeps teachers and learners separated from each other in terms of communication, it is interesting to look at his proposal for a 'grammar-implicit' and co-operative **work programme** for effective MFL classroom business:

- listening to the foreign language;
- using the foreign language;
- asking and answering questions in the foreign language;
- engaging in dramatic activities;
- increasing active/passive vocabularies;
- reading silently;
- relating the language to its social/cultural context;
- doing written work of an error-avoiding (ability-building) nature;
- NB **banning grammar explanation** and **translation**!

Of the matters discussed in this section so far, I feel that most of them have been addressed in a genuine and satisfactory way in my action research on G-I. However, there are three matters in particular which I feel I have overlooked to some degree and which I would be keen to carry forward for G-I treatment in my practice. They are:

1. the natural use of **impromptu speech** among classroom learners and in interaction with the teacher;

2. the use of **reading materials** for **private**, **silent** and **sustained reading** purposes;

3. the **removal of the graded, prescribed, pedagogical grammar agenda**, which I and my colleagues kept intact during our departmental action research.

The G-I teaching approach used by the AR teaching team

The matters outlined above form an essential part of a sensible plan of action for a classroom-based methodological project, specifically G-I. Accordingly, they have returned my attention to my project and to my continuing dialogue with my colleagues. With the wisdom of hindsight their views on G-I teaching and learning have been explained to me in shared discussions, post AR, as follows:

112 — REFLECTIONS ON GRAMMAR-IMPLICIT LANGUAGE TEACHING

- G-I teaching is one thing in theory, another thing in practice. This is the first simple and stark truth!

- Intellectually you find yourself applauding it as a principle but lacking the self-confidence and *savoir-faire* to mobilise it in sustained terms in practice.

- You have to condemn the **irony** of a situation built around an ambitious MFL teaching plan (G-I) which is not provided for in the appropriate terms of time, personnel and resources. Equally you have to condemn the **arrogance** of a system that imposes such an inadequately resourced agenda on to the shoulders of others. For the L2 to be staged and managed in the manner of the L1, similar types of conditions must be applied to serve it and make natural development possible.

- You have to have classes which allow such teaching/learning styles to be put in place as policy. This involves educating pupils on their roles as responsible learners. Teachers pass the *bâton* of subject-knowledge on to the learners who themselves must make a successful changeover, converting matter taught into matter learnt and investing this knowledge in achievement, ultimately. In the existing climate, many classes would not tolerate the G-I method, as one which asks a great deal, or too much, of them. Those classes which are possibly characterised by levels of bad behaviour, or very low ability or low self-esteem, find that their attitudes conspire against their chances to make progress. G-I requires high levels of **concentration** and **participation**.

- The modern languages subject has a number of characteristics which by nature or by degree set it apart from other subjects, e.g.:
  - the ways in which it is expected to be taught and learnt;
  - the amounts of immediate concentration required of the learners;
  - the large input required by the learners;
  - the nature of the input required of the learners;
  - the inability to use the 'back burner' and put off doing the work until another occasion;
  - the importance of training the **memory** in order that knowledge can be accrued for recall and application (this is seen as irksome);
  - the absence of English as the conveyor and purveyor of the subject;
  - the degree of subject difficulty which makes it impossible to 'coast' in this subject and cram knowledge later;
  - the degree of difficulty which makes it easier to opt out than press on;
  - the need for excellent, sustaining classroom relationships, etc.

- The modern languages classroom, typically, suffers from overpopulation! Class sizes need to be reduced quite dramatically anyway. This need becomes all the more urgent if the aims of the NC are to be properly addressed and met.

- We carried out our methodological trials at a moment which was both propitious and unpropitious for the purpose:
  - propitious in terms of anticipating the NC's arrival, just in time, as we thought, for being on line;
  - unpropitious, because the new custom-designed coursebooks were not yet ready (we had no money anyway) and we co-ordinated our work with the help of the existing ones. Despite our making many of our own materials, the standardising coursebooks which we used influenced, i.e. affected, our levels of flexibility and our relationships with G-I. Indeed, for those who were less impassioned than I was on the importance of the AR, the arguably explicit pro-grammar (and ordinarily much-valued) *Tricolore* course neutralised their efforts with the practical G-I trial. It frustrated their intention to remain in control of the G-I principle.

- New coursebooks which we have used since 1994 would have shed a different light on the planning and delivering of G-I. Currently we are using *Francoscope à la mode* in the department. After working from it for a while, you suddenly realise that it has a covert approach to grammar-teaching, although it offers a grammar/verb appendix which is explicit and delivered in English. However, the GCSE will reward with high grades only those candidates who demonstrate correct use of tenses, as before. Time will tell whether we manage to acquire all we need for our purposes from the new publications. We will discover whether the new syllabi, teaching methods, learning strategies, courses and materials will prove worthy of the hope and confidence which we invest in them.

- Without appropriately designed materials, the work on G-I during the AR had been extremely difficult to prepare. Very often it had not been successfully conceived and executed, with the result that the teachers had become increasingly frustrated, disappointed and obsessed with a sense of their own inadequacy.

- There was agreement that the target language should be used as the medium as well as the substance of lessons. We all agreed that we now should adhere to this. We were confident that our learners would accept the situation more and more and finally accept this as the way things are done in the teaching of a foreign language: as policy, therefore.

- There was understanding that words become language when articulated by grammar. Therefore there was agreement that the target language would carry its own grammar, i.e. syllabus, to the learners who were exposed to it. They, in their turn, should go part-way to meet it. Persuaded that the pedagogical grammar is carried on the full linguistical grammar of the language being taught, we concurred on the principle that it must be raised to the learners' consciousness. In this we were contradicting the NC's preference that the FL grammar should not be graded or sequenced, but we were acknowledging the difficulty of addressing a **natural** language agenda in **unnatural** circumstances.

- Further to this and speaking for themselves, the colleagues agreed, however, that they would explain grammar points if asked to. A learner, they believe, has the right to ask: 'Why?' and a teacher has the responsibility to reply in such a way as to satisfy the learner's curiosity and to enable understanding of the issue questioned, even if this entails resorting to explicit explanation in the L1.

- There was the shared opinion that learners nowadays have very little knowledge of or awareness of language, including their native language. Therefore we were confident that our G-I pursuits would not often be disrupted by the question: 'Why?' and the need to address it explicitly. Much of their FL acquisition would be achieved through word and word-cluster learning and the devices of imitation and analogy-making. We reflected on Krashen's views on the attitudes to grammar of the adolescent learner and the absence of a 'carry forward' principle in practical and integrative terms.

- We admitted to looking forward with shared enthusiasm to the time when a formal grammar syllabus would be re-introduced to the English classroom. We felt that the outlook for successful MFL teaching and learning would quickly benefit from this and, in the course of time, the subject would rise in the general performance and esteem levels of its learners. In the meantime, and wryly, we noted that in our local context, at least, our learners' apparently limited and imperfect English did not seem to impede their success in the English Language and English Literature GCSEs!

- Furthermore, until time should bring desired improvements, our modern languages classrooms currently were witnessing too much disruptive behaviour for really satisfactory G-I teaching and learning to take place. (This complaint keeps returning to the discussion! It is placed here as a general observation rather than as one made specifically with the AR in mind.)

- Finally, and to give our considered direct answer to the question on methodological preferences, we said 'Yes' to the 'grammar-implicit' method and the target language approach. **However, despite my own AR conclusion concerning the relative value and use of the factor X, my colleagues preferred to acknowledge the factor X as a desirable and efficacious principle and method support, which they intended to preserve for use in their practice, though not for all occasions, i.e. not wastefully.**

Final personal reflections

The 'grammar-implicit' method of teaching a foreign language is focused on providing relevance, motivation and flexibility and enabling discernible progress for learners. If the G-I movement goes well, learners should see more personal FL progression in relation to their time and effort than has perhaps been the case so far. This would be a welcome development, judging by the press that the subject is receiving at this present time of writing. Even on opening only one MFL update, the EXTRA of the *TES* of 10 October 1997, I read (as doubtless do many other people, with recognition and concern regarding the situations depicted) about the following:

- the reluctance of the British 'to have a go in other languages' due to a national 'lack of confidence';
- Eddie Ross's belief that language teaching is heading for a crisis of falling standards, twinned with his concern that
- 'classes are wasted in the constant struggle to maintain discipline'.

There is still everything to prove where MFL is concerned in National Curriculum terms and times. It will be interesting to see whether the new methods, as teachers interpret them, are able to bring good results for learners. Already the GCSE results of 1998 and 1999 have produced evidence to aid analysis and discussion of the inherent issues. Meanwhile, we hardly need to be reminded that schools (teachers and learners) have suffered a great deal of educational change over the last years. The reactions which are generated in the classrooms currently may be in part the expression of learners' responses to so much change and reform. Reaction was to be expected, whether or not this has been exacerbated by other stresses and influences prevailing in the world of the learner. If change which has become a habit were to break its pattern for a while, we could usefully evaluate in the time ahead the position and effect of the advocated MFL teaching strategies in current times and seek to perfect our expertise in employing those strategies in our classrooms. **We need also to assess the effects and implications of the pre-16 MFL teaching and learning strategies on the post-16 practice, itself undergoing measures of change and re-styling as we reflect at this time of writing.**

At a personal level, I now know certain things about my own relationship with the 'grammar implicit' approach. Thanks to my action research and the reflection on practice that I did at that time and have attempted to continue with since then, I know that I have unfinished business with it. My intention now is to return to the drawing board to re-examine the G-I concept with certain adjustments, refinements and embellishments in mind and on the strength of certain extended insights of my own, won through my continued post-AR reflection. Then on to the classroom's front line again, possibly for a further investigative effort!

Endpiece

'Classroom research ... embraces a substantial section of my time-tabled work at school, which means that a daily amount of time is given to the project by myself and colleagues in my department, regularly, reliably and unavoidably.'
(Margaret Wells, *Reflections on Practice 1*, p.11)

'I now know more about grammar teaching ... I have discovered more about myself as a teacher, as a departmental manager and as a person, as my research has proceeded.'
(*Reflections on Practice 1*, p.56)

'At a personal level, I now know certain things about my own relationship with the "grammar implicit" approach. Thanks to my action research ... I know that I have unfinished business with it. My intention is now to return to the drawing board ...'
(present text, p.116).

Some five years span these reflections by Margaret Wells on implicit grammar teaching. A thread common to all three is, very evidently, one of deep and enthusiastic engagement, with her curiosity serving to sustain a very substantial endeavour. Equally clear are also the continuing fascination she describes in relation to particular features of the work itself and her persistent sense of gain. As principal motivator and actor in the project, she is fully entitled to make such a claim. Her book nonetheless displays consistent generosity towards those colleagues who took part in her enquiry and who were similarly stimulated and ultimately changed by that participation.

It is thus a first and great pleasure for an editor of one of the books in the *Reflections on Practice* series to be able to highlight the fulfilment in this present book of the optimism which has marked every stage of Margaret's longitudinal project; also to welcome the insights and surprises provided by her own and her associates' careful enquiries.

It is important to stress the surprises. Typically, both the outcomes of reflection on practice and the process itself are prone to differ from what is expected at the outset by those conducting an enquiry. The effects of such unpredictability are often both problematical and energising. Margaret herself puts the point as follows:

> 'I had entered the contrastive study with an open mind. However, ... pressed to give my personal view on which of my two trialled methods would emerge as the more effective, I chose M2 ... It promised to be an interesting exercise.' (present text, p.96)

Significant changes in the anticipated enquiry process also had to be made. The potential classroom enquirer is often put off by worries about not being sure enough at the outset quite where things will lead. On the contrary, in the most searching investigations such as the one recounted here, open-mindedness is not just a hallmark but a condition of success. Margaret has quite evidently done any such doubters a big service by showing this to be so.

It is a point of view which Antony Peck and I strove to emphasise when we edited the first title in this series. So long as the questions to which answers are sought are immediately clear, the work will have its focus. A little help may be required in choosing, at least initially, the most appropriate ways of gathering evidence; also (as we wrote) 'the skills of reflection ... improve with practice' (*Language teaching in the mirror*, p.71). Two very striking features of Margaret's work have in fact been its adaptability under changing constraints and its consistency of purpose. She has demonstrated an iron determination to know more about teaching and learning processes in relation to foreign language grammar and has refused to lose sight of that goal, however much she has adapted the means and the course of her research.

It is hoped that Margaret's persistence and her ability to overcome unpredicted obstacles, as well as her evident intellectual and professional excitement, will serve as an encouragement to others – particularly for exploration of less ambitious issues than those surrounding 'grammar'. If she has been able to carry through a three-year-plus longitudinal study of this complex topic without flagging, then there is surely hope for the rest of us in our smaller-scale reflective enquiries!

A feature of Margaret's work which is partly evident in Chapter 3, and which some may feel less inclined to emulate, is the weight she attached to reading around her subject. (See Appendix B for the tip of this particular iceberg!) That aspect has always been a vital one for her, as grammar is a topic on which many have had their say in the past as well as one which draws heavily on theory. The breadth of Margaret's reading certainly provides a reassuringly solid basis for her work, as Peter Neil's did for his thorough investigation of teaching through the target language in the fourth book (*Reflections on the target language*). It is worth stressing, however, that few topics need as much underpinning of this kind; and no one should be deterred by fears to the contrary. Preliminary (or simultaneous) reading is like one's choice of enquiry methods; both depend on the topic and both are most effective when simply appropriate to the task, rather than 'correct' in any general sense or complex for the sake of respectability.

At any event, some of the main 'outcomes' or insights provided by Margaret's work will no doubt seem at least as reassuring to others as they have been somewhat unexpected to her. Difficult though it was for her (and her colleagues) strictly to maintain the distinction between the two 'methods' contrasted, her conclusions tend to endorse the advantages of much current practice. That is, in contextualising and implicitly demonstrating points of grammar to be taught and learned, rather than going back to explicit formulations (even as retrospective summaries). The latter seem to have provided little help even to pupils who, on other criteria, may (arguably) have been more able to handle such abstractions. **The pupils seem to have learned from what they did with the language rather than from what they were told about it. That is very well worth remembering.**

Further practical reassurance may well be found, too, in the perspective which Margaret has developed in respect of the whole concept of teaching 'methods'. The limited success over the years of successive methodological revolutions may pre-dispose any of us to accept the argument that other professional qualities such as a teacher's styles of work, or the relationships s/he creates within a class, are of greater significance than a method of whatever hue. It is good to find such a humane perspective confidently emerging from such a rigorous and extensive study.

While Margaret herself writes of applying herself now to further 'refinements and embellishments' in her own practice of a grammar-implicit approach, what can other MFL teachers take from the study and the approaches it uses? Some answers have already been provided: to do with encouragement for teachers to enquire into practical issues of personal interest, with the relatively easy acquisition and practice of relevant enquiry skills and with the virtues of open-mindedness in pursuit of greater understanding.

Another aspect which should not be ignored concerns the benefits, individual and reciprocal, of teaming up with others to undertake curiosity-driven reflection, e.g. within a department, as Margaret did, or even across institutions. Margaret recounts a developing involvement among her colleagues which, though fraught at times, was ultimately beneficial and sustaining. An example of cross-institutional co-operation (in local Sixth Form Colleges) can be found in the second book in this series (*Reflections on reading*, edited by Michael Grenfell) where Liliane White reports a collaborative study of 'A' level literary reading. Then again, the theme of support within and beyond the walls of one school may itself become a part of the focus of enquiry, as it did for several writers in the third book (*Reflections on modern languages in primary education*, edited by Alison Hurrell and Peter Satchwell).

The *Reflections on Practice* series, in the way it was conceived and in what it has already achieved, seeks to encourage language teachers to engage in what Antony Peck and I described in the first book (*Language teaching in the mirror,* p.71) as 'some systematic reflection in a more down-to-earth, matter of fact way'

– a form of enquiry, that is, which is less separately carried out than by outsider-researchers looking into our classrooms, and which harnesses insider knowledge to the informed pursuit of answers reflective teachers themselves want to hear about.

We knew there would be value in sharing more widely in print insights perhaps already being networked on a local basis. We explicitly foresaw a wide range of issues being addressed and shared in this way. Margaret Wells is to be congratulated on making clearly available to a professional readership the fruits of her own complex and extended study.

David Westgate

Appendix A

Samples of the AR pupils' creative work

Sample One – *Poème*
Gâteau (11 G-E and 11 G-I)

Aujourd'hui nous avons appris
Comment faire un bon gâteau;
Nous savons y mettre beaucoup de choses
Pour le rendre fin et beau.
Les ingrédients ... beaucoup! beaucoup! ...
Dans cette liste je vous les raconte presque tous:
De la farine, des œufs, de l'essence de vanille,
Des noix de noyer, des raisins secs, du sirop doux,
Des fruits frais, comme bananes – oh, c'est facile!
Mettez-les, en mélange, peut-être aussi des épices,
Pour lui donner – (à ce gâteau) – un très, très bon goût.
Faites dans une moule!
Mettez au four!
Attendez – une heure – ce dessert du jour!

Quel beau gâteau!
Qui l'a fait? ... Tu l'as fait? Toi?
Non, Peter en est responsable cette fois.
Qu'il l'a bien fait! Les filles de classe K aussi:
Kirsty et Kelly et leurs efforts et soucis,
Et nous autres. Quels gâteaux préférons-nous?
Ceux au chocolat? A la vanille? A l'amande?
Celui à la crème profonde ou celui aux bananes?
On aime chacun et on les aime tous.
Tu fais des gâteaux tous les jours, mon ami?
Tu vas en faire demain? La semaine prochaine?
Une torte simple ou sophistiquée? Une torte belle?
Tu feras un gâteau anglais pour Noël? ...

Moi, je fais des gâteaux de temps en temps,
Mais, d'habitude j'y assiste: j'aide maman
A faire des choses bien délicieuses
Pour notre famille, qui les mange et ...
Reste ainsi satisfaite et heureuse.

Pour la classe G-E:

A chaque vers de ce poème il y a de la grammaire.
Trouvez-la et indiquez si vous savez comment faire.
Le gâteau même est délicieux. Prenez-en! Mangez bien!
On vous souhaite bon appétit:
Laissez aucune tranche pour demain!

Faire un Gâteau: le Procédé et le Produit

A. LES INGRÉDIENTS (LA RECETTE: EXEMPLE)

175 grammes de beurre
120 mls de sirop (mélasse)
2 œufs (grand modèle)
150 mls de confiture d'oranges
350 grammes de farine
5 mls (une petite cuiller) de levure
150 mls de lait
50 grammes de bananes écrasées
de la muscade
de la cannelle
du cognac
de l'eau
des clous de girofle

B. MÉTHODE = COMMENT FAIRE

(i) *Les impléments (les outils)*

Un four
Une moule à gâteau
Des cuillers (à thé, à soupe, à dessert)
Un bol

(ii) *Méthode: Action*

1. Graissez la moule!
2. Prenez le bol!
3. Mettez le beurre dans le bol!
4. Ajoutez-y le sirop et frappez bien!
5. Fouettez les œufs!
6. Ajoutez-les peu à peu ... au mélange dans le bol!
7. Joignez-y une moitié de la confiture et toute la farine avec les épices, les bananes et le lait!
8. Mêlez tout ça et mettez dans la moule!

(iii) *Méthode: Derniers pas*

1. Mettez le gâteau dans le four (au four)!
2. Vous devez utiliser le centre four et une chaleur moyenne (= 180°C/N°.4)
3. Il vous faut faire cuire le gâteau pendant une heure.
4. Pour décorer et compléter le gâteau vous allez finalement le couronner des cornflakes (paillettes de maïs), du sirop et de la confiture, qui restent.

Exercises (étudiez le poème pour trouver les résponses)

I. Repondez aux questions suivantes:
   1. Qui a fait le gâteau dans le poème?
   2. Comment trouves-tu ce gâteau?
   3. Quelle sorte de gâteau préfères-tu?
   4. Tu as fait un gâteau récemment? Décris-le!
   5. Tu vas faire un gâteau ce weekend? Explique!
   6. Qui fait les gâteaux chez toi d'habitude?
   7. Quand? Où? Comment?
   8. Qui n'aime pas manger les gâteaux chez toi?
   9. Quels gâteaux aimes-tu le mieux/le pire?
   10. Fais la description du dernier gâteau que tu as mangé.

II. Etudiez le texte du poeme. Trouvez les expressions qui suivent et faites des phrases qui les contiennent:

(i) aujourd'hui (ii) bon (iii) beaucoup de (iv) tous (v) de la (vi) des (vi) de l' (vii) du (ix) lui (x) ce (xi) quelle (xii) qui (xiii) profonde (xiv) demain (xv) la semaine prochaine (xvi) de temps en temps

III. Etudiez le texte du poeme. Trouvez des expressions qui conviennent aux categories ci-dessous:
   (a) expressions de description/qualité
   (b) expressions d'action
   (c) expressions de nom
   (d) expressions de quantité
   (e) expressions de circonstances
   (f) expressions de temps présent, futur, passé

Sample Two – *Rendez-vous surprise*

RENDEZ-VOUS-SURPRISE (EXTRAIT)

Cilla   Quel bon accueil!

Salut tout le monde! Vous êtes les bienvenus à Rendez-vous surprise. Et nous avons trois belles jeunes filles qui attendent avec impatience leur opportunité de faire rendez-vous avec un jeune homme ce soir. Et les voilà, les filles! Entrez les filles!

Nous avons _____ de _____.

Nous avons _____ de _____.

et nous avons _____ de _____.

Elles sont vraiment très jolies, n'est-ce pas?

Allons! Parlons tout de suite avec elles.

Bonsoir, les filles!

Filles   Bonsoir, Cilla!

Cilla   Dites donc, Numéro Un, vous êtes vraiment jolie! Dites-nous, s'il vous plaît, qui êtes vous et d'où venez-vous? Que faites-vous dans la vie? Et quelle sorte de jeunes hommes préfèrez-vous?

Nº 1   Bonjour, Cilla. Je m'appelle _____.

Pour gagner ma vie je travaille comme _____.

Je préfere les jeunes hommes qui portent les blue jeans, surtout _____ il est très beau.

Cilla   Et vous, Numéro Deux. Quel beau chapeau!

Que vous êtes belle. Vous aimez les chapeaux?

Vous les faites de vos propres mains? Vous pourriez m'en faire un? Pour le prochain mariage de deux participants de *'Blind Date'*?

Nº 2   Bien sûr! Oui, Cilla. Je vous ferai un nouveau chapeau, beaucoup meilleur que votre dernier chapeau. Je le ferai des boîtes en carton, tout simplement.

Cilla   Comment vous appelez-vous, Numéro Deux? Et d'où venez-vous?

Nº.2   Je m'appelle _____ Cilla, èt je viens de _____.

Cilla	Et que faites-vous dans la vie?
No.2	Je suis _____ Cilla. J'aime beaucoup faire mon travail. Et je rêve de J.C.V.D. Il est le meilleur, lui.
Cilla	Et vous, Numéro Trois. Que vous êtes attirante!
No.3	Merci, Cilla.
Cilla	Vous aimez faire le ski, je crois.
No.3	Oui, Cilla, c'est vrai.
Cilla	Vous avez un sens d'aventure?
No.3	Oui, c'est correct.
Cilla	Comment vous appelez-vous? Et d'où venez-vous, Numéro Trois?
No.3	Je m'appelle _____ Cilla, et j'habite à _____.
Cilla	Avec qui voulez-vous faire des aventures, Numéro Trois?
No.3	Avec Robin Williams, Cilla. Il a un très bon sens d'humeur. Il me fait rire.
Cilla	Et que faites-vous pour gagner la vie?
No.3	Je suis étudiante à l'université de Newcastle, Cilla, la ville de ma naissance.
Cilla	Très bien, Numéro Trois; très bien toutes les filles. Je vous souhaite toutes beaucoup de plaisir en jouant à 'Blind Date' 'Rendez-vous surprise' ce soir. Amusez-vous bien.
Filles	Merci, Cilla. Merci beaucoup.
Cilla	Alors, nous avons voyagé à Bruxelles chercher un jeune homme pour jouer à 'Blind Date'. Et le voilà! Je vous présente Max. Entrez donc, Max. Bonsoir, Max, Salut! Comment ça va?
Max	Ça va bien, Cilla, merci.
Cilla	Vous parlez très bien le français, Max – un très bon accent.
Max	Merci, Cilla.
Cilla	Vous parlez plusieurs langues étrangères en fait, n'est-ce pas?
Max	Oui, Cilla, sept en fait: l'anglais, le français, l'allemand et l'espagnol y compris.

Cilla	Formidable! Maintenant on attend votre première question, Max.
Max	D'accord, Cilla. Bonsoir les filles!
Filles	Bonsoir, monsieur. Bonsoir, Max.
Max	Ma première question à vous toutes. Moi, je suis un vrai européen, citoyen du Pays Bas, né en Belgique et maintenant habitant de la Grande Bretagne. Je voudrais savoir si vous aussi êtes de vraies européennes, et de quelle façon? Cette question à vous, d'abord, Numéro Un. (continued)

Rendez-vous surprise (Exercises)

Faites les exercices suivants.

1. Je me présente. Donnez dix détails:
   nom / addresse / âge / loisirs / rêves / une histoire drôle / voyages, etc.
2. Posez des questions à votre copain qui joue le rôle de 'Max' (cinq questions).
3. Imaginez le jeune homme/la jeune femme qui vient chercher un partenaire pour faire rendez-vous. Décrivez-le/la.
4. Imaginez les trois autres participants qui se présentent et veulent être choisis comme partenaire. Décrivez-les.
5. Choisissez un voyage pour le couple.
   Décrivez-le et donnez vos raisons pour expliquer ce choix.
6. Décrivez un bon rappport et un mauvais rapport entre les deux jeunes participants.
   Qu'est-ce qu'ils ont dit après, l'un de l'autre en chaque cas?

Sample Three – *Poème*
Premier Amour (Year 11 – Kate)

Même si j'avais su que ça deviendrait triste,
Chaque fois que j'ai vu ton image au loin
Avec quel plaisir et sans hésiter, moi,
J'aurais couru pour te voir à chaque coin.

Car
En toi j'ai vu la création du monde;
En toi j'ai connu le bonheur;
En toi j'ai eu une expérience profonde;
En toi j'ai perdu mon cœur.

Toi
Tu es le vent qui chasse dans ma voile,
Le soleil qui parcourt mon feuillage,
Je ferais tout, oui, pour t'avoir
Car, moi, je suis tout à fait folle.
Car, moi, je ne suis pas du tout sage,
Je mourrais donc, oui, pour te voir …

Ah!
La vérité est simple
Et claire comme le nouveau jour;
Si j'avais vu … si j'avais su
Que j'aurais le cœur battu,
Que je perdrais mon extase jamais,
Que mon émotion ne disparaîtrait …
Si j'avais su
Que la vie serait vide sans toi,
Que la vie serait vide pour moi …
Si j'avais vu
La futilité et le désespoir!

Maintenant
La terre sous mes pieds disparaît
Le ciel au dessus de ma tête est noir
Mon amour est parti
Je ne peux plus le voir …
Inutile de me plaindre et de protester.
Si j'avais vu, si j'avais su
Ce qui se passerait,
Je n'aurais rien dit, je n'aurais rien fait.
Rien n'aurait pu changer ma destinée.

Appendix B

A selection of key background sources

Brumfit, C J (1984) Communicative methodology in language teaching, Cambridge University Press.
Dodson, C J (1967) *Language teaching and the bilingual method*, Pitman and Sons Ltd.
Ellis, R (1984) *Classroom second language development*, Pergamon Press Ltd.
Halliwell, S (1993) *Grammar matters,* Pathfinder 17, CILT.
Hawkins, E W (1981) *Modern languages in the curriculum*, Cambridge University Press.
Heafford, M (March, 1993) 'What is grammar, who is she?' in *Language Learning Journal 7*, pp.55–58.
Johnstone, R (1987), *A handbook on communicative methodology in foreign language teaching*, Stirling: Department of Education Stirling.
King, L and Boaks, P (eds) (1994) *Grammar! A conference report*, CILT.
Krashen, S D (1981) *Second language acquisition and second language learning*, Pergamon, Oxford.
Krashen, S D and Terrell, T D (1983) *The natural approach: Language acquisition in the classroom*, Hayward, California, Alemany Press.
Littlewood, W T (1981) *Communicative language teaching,* Cambridge University Press.
McArthur, T (1983) *A foundation course for language teachers*, Cambridge University Press.
Mitchell, R (1988) *Communicative language teaching in practice*, CILT.
Richards, J C and Rodgers, T S (1986) *Approaches and methods in language teaching*, Cambridge University Press.
Rivers, W M (1983) *Communicating naturally in a second language: Theory and practice in language teaching*, Cambridge University Press.
Rivers, W M (ed) (1987) *Interactive language teaching,* Cambridge University Press.
Rutherford, W E (1987) *Second language grammar: Learning and Teaching*, Longman Group UK Ltd.
Sharwood Smith, M (1981) 'Consciousness raising and the second language learner' in *Applied linguistics*, Vol II, No. 2, pp.159–168.
Schräder-Neff, R D (1976, 1st edn) *Schüler lernen Lernen*, Beltz Praxis.
Wilkins, D A (1974, 1979) *Second language learning and teaching*, Edward Arnold.
Wilkinson, A (1971) *The foundations of language*, Oxford University Press.